FoundHER:

Navigating the Path to Empowerment, Success, and Entrepreneurial Triumph for Women

Melissa Seymour

ISBN: 9798866472949

Dedication

To my sisters—the dreamers, the change makers, the inventors, creators, doers, inspirers, and shape shifters. May this book be your north star along your Founders journey, informing you of the guidelines we must all follow in pursing our dreams. May it inform you so you never have to be a young entrepreneur like me, wasting hundreds of thousands of dollars on rooms full of male suits, telling me what I should do, often against my better judgement. This is the book I wish I had as a resource—I would have trusted and backed myself because of the knowledge imparted in these pages. May you do the same. x

To my courageous and inspiring budding entrepreneur, Saskia. My teenage daughter who has already founded her own fashion label (at 16). May you keep dreaming, climbing and creating, my darling. I love you with every fiber of my being and I will have your back every step of your way (or as long as you'll have me!)

I've had two publishing contracts with major publishers and after reading about Taylor Swift's disruption to the film industry with her Eras Tour film, I decided to be brave like her and bring this book directly to the platforms that sell it. Publishers said it would take months to traditionally publish this, but with the options available to self-publish and keep the majority of the profits, I thought—why wait? So here you go...

CONTENTS

Introduction

In the grand tapestry of life, we often find that it's not our moments of success, but rather our moments of struggle and resilience, that truly define us. We learn and grow not in the easy stretches of our journey, but in the valleys of challenge and adversity. And it is in these valleys that we find the radiant light of our inner strength, shining brighter than ever before.

As you hold *FoundHER* in your hands, I invite you to embark on a transformative journey—a journey that celebrates the spirit of female entrepreneurship, resilience, and unbreakable determination. This book is more than just a guide; it's a testament to the unwavering human spirit, a source of inspiration, and a call to action for women who aspire to create their own destinies.

My own path to entrepreneurship has been a series of trials and triumphs, with the most profound lessons learned in the depths of failure. I've often found that I've learned more from the setbacks, the stumbles, and the moments when the odds seemed insurmountable than I ever did from the soaring highs of success.

But my journey hasn't been defined by business alone. Alongside my entrepreneurial pursuits, I've faced another formidable challenge—a battle with my own health. Not once, not twice, but three times, I've undergone brain surgeries, each an arduous test of my physical and emotional resilience. I also battled with Bacterial Meningitis after my first one, which was a life-or-death experience. These experiences could have been the end of my story, but instead, they became the chapters that illustrated my capacity to rise above adversity.

In the midst of these health battles, life dealt another crushing blow—the dissolution of a 20-year marriage—while I was recovering from my last brain surgery. With two children. With 100% custody. The pain and heartache of such an ordeal could have extinguished my light, leaving me in the shadows of despair—and it did, for a while. But then, it became the catalyst for a profound transformation, illuminating my path forward.

Throughout all these challenges, my light has not dimmed—it has grown stronger, brighter (even though it flickered at times), and more resilient. I am not defined by my setbacks; I am defined by my ability to overcome them, and I stand here today to share the invaluable lessons I've gathered along the way.

FoundHER is an homage to the indomitable spirit of women everywhere. It's a testament to the belief that within each of us resides the power to rise, to rebuild, and to reignite our passion. Together, we will explore the principles of entrepreneurship, leadership, and personal growth that have guided me through the darkest of times and propelled me toward the brightest of futures.

Dear reader, you hold the key to your own journey of discovery, transformation, and success. Let *FoundHER* be your guide, your source of inspiration, and your beacon of hope as you embark on a path of self-discovery, resilience, and empowerment. Together, let us rise above, unleash our strength, and thrive in a world where anything is possible.

x Melissa

Chapter 1:
Sparking Your Creative Genius

Welcome to the journey of self-discovery and innovation. In this chapter, I'll embark on a profound exploration of your inner innovator, tapping into your innate creativity and entrepreneurial spirit. These insights will be instrumental in not only sparking your imagination but also aligning your passions and purpose with your business idea. Passion is the heartbeat of innovation and entrepreneurship. By tapping into what genuinely excites and motivates you, you'll lay the foundation for a business idea that not only thrives but also fulfills your soul.

Passion is the driving force behind innovation. In this section, I'll delve into the concept of passion and its pivotal role in cultivating creativity.

Before I dive into the techniques, let's first understand what passion truly means. Passion isn't just a fleeting interest; it's a deep, burning desire that drives you to action. It's the force that keeps you committed, even when faced with challenges.

Your entrepreneurial journey begins with self-discovery. To discover your passions, you must embark on a journey of introspection. Here, I'll guide you through techniques that reach deep into your psyche:

1. Journaling as a Path to Self-Discovery: Journaling isn't merely about documenting your day; it's a tool for understanding your thoughts, emotions, and desires.

2. Stream-of-Consciousness Writing: Dive deep into your stream of consciousness. Write freely, without judgment or censorship. This practice can reveal hidden desires and interests that your conscious mind might overlook.

3. Visionary Journaling: Use your journal to envision your ideal life and business. Explore questions like, "What would I do if I knew I couldn't fail?" and "What legacy do I want to leave behind?" to uncover your deepest aspirations.

4. The Power of Self-Reflection: Self-reflection is the mirror through which you gain insight into your true self. Here are some self-reflection techniques to help you identify your passions and delve deeper into your business idea.

The Socratic Method

Named after the ancient Greek philosopher Socrates, the Socratic Method is a powerful tool in exploring your passions and business ideas because it fosters critical thinking, challenges assumptions, clarifies concepts, and promotes self-discovery. By using open-ended questions to guide discussions, individuals and teams can navigate the complexities of entrepreneurship, innovate, and make well-informed decisions that lead to the development of successful business ideas and strategies. I'll explore this further as I'm a big believer of using this technique as it's helped my teams and I in identifying business opportunities and navigating business challenges.

- Philosophical Foundation

The Socratic Method is rooted in the belief that knowledge is best acquired through active, open-ended questioning and critical thinking rather than passive acceptance of information.

- Open-Ended Questions

In the context of business, the Socratic Method involves asking open-ended questions that encourage individuals or teams to think deeply about a particular topic or problem. These questions often start with "What," "Why," "How," or "Can you explain?"

- Exploring Assumptions

One of the primary objectives of the Socratic Method is to challenge and explore assumptions. In business, this is crucial because assumptions can lead to faulty strategies and decisions. By asking questions like, "What assumptions are we making?" or "Why do we believe this to be true?" individuals and teams can uncover hidden biases and potential pitfalls.

- Clarifying Concepts

The method also aims to clarify concepts and definitions. For instance, if a business idea is being discussed, the Socratic Method might involve questions like "How do we define success in this context?" or "What does innovation mean for our organization?"

- Promoting Critical Thinking

Socratic questioning is designed to stimulate critical thinking and reasoned judgment. By continually asking questions that require thoughtful responses, individuals are encouraged to consider multiple perspectives, weigh evidence, and make well-informed decisions.

- Encouraging Self-Discovery

In the Socratic Method, the emphasis is on self-discovery, which will lead to revelations about your passions. Instead of providing answers, a facilitator (or oneself) uses questions to guide the exploration of ideas. This process often leads to a deeper understanding of the subject matter and personal insights.

- Iterative Process

The Socratic Method is an iterative process. As answers to questions are provided, further questions are asked to delve deeper into the topic. This iterative nature allows for a comprehensive examination of ideas.

When exploring your business idea, challenge your assumptions and beliefs through Socratic questioning. To get started, ask yourself probing questions like, "Why do I feel drawn to this?" or "What does success mean to me?" to gain clarity on your passions.

1. Past-Present-Future Reflection: Examine your past experiences, your present interests, and your future aspirations. Identify common threads and recurring themes that can lead you to your true passions.

2. The Exploration Mindset: To discover your passion, you must be open to exploration. Don't limit yourself to what

you already know; venture into new territories and experiences. Attend workshops, take classes, or engage in hobbies you've never considered before. Often, your true passion lies in the uncharted.

3. Seeking Inspiration from Others: Conversations with passionate individuals can spark your own passions. Engage in discussions with people from diverse backgrounds and industries. Listen intently to their stories and experiences. You might find inspiration and new interests in their journeys.

4. Passion Projects and Mini Experiments: Sometimes, the best way to discover your passion is by doing. Create small passion projects or experiments to test your interests. This hands-on approach can provide insights into what truly excites you.

5. Overcoming Fear and Limiting Beliefs: Fear and self-doubt can often obscure your passions. Techniques such as positive affirmations, visualization, and cognitive restructuring can help you break free from limiting beliefs.

Chapter 2:
Defining Your Entrepreneurial Purpose

Purpose is the guiding star of entrepreneurship. A clear and compelling purpose not only fuels your determination but also serves as a magnetic force, drawing customers, partners, and supporters who resonate with your mission. In this chapter, I will embark on a journey with you to define your entrepreneurial purpose in a way that ignites passion and fuels innovation.

Section 1: The Power of Purpose

Before I delve into the exercises, let's understand why defining your purpose is essential:

1. Aligning Your North Star: Your purpose is your North Star. It provides direction, ensuring that every decision and action aligns with your mission and values. It keeps you on course when faced with challenges and uncertainties.

2. Inspiring Passion and Resilience: A compelling purpose inspires passion. When you're deeply connected to your purpose, you're more likely to persevere through

adversity and maintain unwavering commitment to your entrepreneurial journey.

3. Attracting Like-Minded Individuals: A clear purpose acts as a beacon, attracting individuals who share your values and vision. It helps you build a supportive network of customers, partners, and collaborators who resonate with what you stand for.

Defining Your Entrepreneurial Purpose

Now, let's dive into purpose-defining exercises that will help you articulate your mission and values:

1. The "Why" Exercise: Start by asking yourself why you want to start this business. Continue to ask "why" several times to dig deeper into your motivations. This technique, often called the "5 Whys," helps uncover the core purpose behind your business idea. (See chapter 5 for details.)

2. Values Clarification: Identify your core values as an entrepreneur. What principles and beliefs drive your decisions? values clarification exercises, such as the "Values Auction" or "Core Values Ranking," can help you prioritize and articulate your values.

3. The Vision Statement: Craft a vision statement that encapsulates your ultimate goal. Use techniques like visualization and future pacing to envision your business's impact in the world. Consider creating a vision board or a vivid narrative of your future success. I've crafted a sample Vision Statement below to inspire yours. (Actually, feel free to copy it.

Sometimes it's easier to start out this way and customize what's already there.)

"At <Your Business Name>, our mission is to empower and uplift through innovation, creativity, and unwavering dedication. Guided by the strength and vision of our female leadership, we are committed to creating a world where every person, regardless of gender, background, or circumstance, has the opportunity to thrive.

We believe that business can be a force for positive change, and we embrace the responsibility to lead with purpose. Our commitment is to:

- *Elevate Women:* We strive to be a beacon of empowerment for women, both within our organization and in the communities we touch. Through mentorship, equal opportunities, and inclusive leadership, we aim to break down barriers and shatter glass ceilings.

- *Drive Innovation:* Innovation is at the core of what we do. We're dedicated to pushing boundaries, exploring new frontiers, and continuously improving our products and services. Our innovation isn't just about products; it's about creating solutions that make a meaningful impact on people's lives.

- *Foster Sustainability:* We recognize the importance of environmental and social sustainability. We are committed to reducing our ecological footprint, supporting ethical practices, and contributing to the well-being of the planet and its inhabitants.

- *Champion Diversity and Inclusion:* Diversity is our strength. We celebrate differences and promote an inclusive culture that values every individual's unique perspective. Through diversity, we drive creativity and innovation.

- *Make a Difference:* Our ultimate goal is to make a positive difference in the lives of our customers, employees, partners, and the global community. We measure success not just in profits but in the positive change we bring about.

- *Lead with Integrity:* Integrity is the foundation of our business. We conduct ourselves with honesty, transparency, and ethical responsibility in all our interactions and decisions.

"At <Your Business Name>, we are not just a business; we are a movement for change. Our purpose-driven approach guides us in every endeavor, and our commitment to a brighter, more equitable future fuels our passion to excel.

Together, with our female-led team, partners, and customers, we are shaping a world where purpose, progress, and prosperity intersect. Join us on this inspiring journey toward a better tomorrow."

This mission statement reflects a commitment to empowerment, innovation, sustainability, diversity, positive impact, integrity, and purpose-driven leadership—a powerful combination for a female-led business with a vision for a brighter future!

4. Stakeholder Mapping: Identify the key stakeholders impacted by your business, including customers, employees, partners, and the community. Explore how your business's purpose can positively affect each group and contribute to their fulfillment in being involved in your venture.

5. Impact Assessment: Analyze the potential positive impact your business can have on society, the environment, or specific causes that matter to you. In today's business environment, this is crucial for attracting the right customers, partners and employees—more and more research into this points to this being a crucial factor in making purchasing and employment decisions. Consider conducting a comprehensive impact assessment using frameworks like the "Triple Bottom Line" or the "Sustainability Impact Assessment." Here are some examples of these:

The "Triple Bottom Line" (TBL) is a framework that goes beyond traditional business metrics to evaluate the performance of a business in three dimensions: social, environmental, and financial. Here's an example of how you can apply the TBL framework when cultivating a new business idea.

Business Idea: An Eco-Friendly Clothing Brand

1. Social Bottom Line

Purpose: The social aspect of the TBL framework focuses on the impact your business idea will have on people and communities.

Example Metrics and Considerations:

- Job Creation: Calculate how many jobs your eco-friendly clothing brand can create in local communities.

- Fair Labor Practices: Ensure that your supply chain adheres to fair labor practices and ethical working conditions.

- Community Engagement: Develop initiatives to engage with and give back to the communities where your business operates, such as supporting local charities or organizing clean-up events.

- Diversity and Inclusion: Implement policies to foster diversity and inclusion within your workforce and customer base.

2. Environmental Bottom Line

Purpose: The environmental aspect focuses on the ecological impact of your business idea and its contribution to sustainability.

Example Metrics and Considerations:

- Carbon Footprint Reduction: Calculate how your clothing brand can reduce carbon emissions through sustainable sourcing, manufacturing, and distribution.

- Waste Reduction: Set targets for reducing waste in the production process and promoting recycling or upcycling of clothing items.

- Sustainable Materials: Source eco-friendly and sustainable materials, such as organic cotton or recycled fabrics.

- Energy Efficiency: Implement energy-efficient practices in your operations, such as using renewable energy sources or optimizing transportation logistics.

3. Financial Bottom Line

Purpose: The financial aspect remains crucial, as it ensures the long-term viability and profitability of your business.

Example Metrics and Considerations:

- Profitability: Create financial projections that demonstrate the potential profitability of your eco-friendly clothing brand.

- Return on Investment (ROI): Calculate the expected ROI for sustainability initiatives, such as investing in energy-efficient equipment or sustainable sourcing practices.

- Cost Management: Develop strategies to manage costs effectively while maintaining high-quality and sustainable products.

- Market Demand: Analyze market trends and demand for eco-friendly clothing to ensure a viable customer base.

By applying the "Triple Bottom Line" framework to your eco-friendly clothing brand, you can evaluate your business idea holistically. This approach ensures that your business not only generates profits but also considers its social and environmental impact. It can be a powerful tool to attract socially-conscious consumers, build a sustainable brand, and contribute positively to society and the environment while achieving financial success.

Alternatively, you can craft a "Sustainability Impact Assessment". Here is an example of one for the same business idea used above—a new sustainable clothing brand. This is an essential step in evaluating and communicating the environmental and social impact of your business.

"Sustainability Impact Assessment" for "Your Sustainable Clothing Brand"

1. Introduction

Provide an overview of your sustainable clothing brand, its mission, and its commitment to environmental and social responsibility.

2. Environmental Impact

    i.   Sustainable Sourcing:

- Describe the materials used in your clothing products, emphasizing sustainable and eco-friendly choices, such as organic cotton, recycled fabrics, or low-impact dyes.

- Assess the environmental impact of your sourcing decisions, including reduced water usage, lower carbon emissions, and decreased chemical usage.

ii. Manufacturing and Production:

- Explain your manufacturing processes and any eco-conscious practices, like energy-efficient machinery or waste reduction strategies.

- Quantify the reduction in greenhouse gas emissions or waste generation resulting from your production methods.

iii. Transportation and Logistics:

- Outline your transportation strategies, including efforts to reduce the carbon footprint of shipping and distribution.

- Calculate the reduction in transportation-related emissions through efficient logistics and distribution channels.

iv. Packaging:

- Detail your packaging choices, highlighting eco-friendly materials and packaging design that minimizes waste.

- Estimate the reduction in packaging waste and the use of sustainable packaging materials.

3. Social Impact

i. Fair Labor Practices:

- Describe your commitment to fair labor practices, including fair wages, safe working conditions, and ethical treatment of workers.

- Provide examples of how your clothing brand supports fair labor practices throughout the supply chain.

ii. Job Creation:

- Report on the number of jobs created, both locally and within the regions where your products are manufactured.

- Highlight any initiatives or partnerships that support job creation, particularly in disadvantaged communities.

iii. Community Engagement:

- Share details of your community engagement efforts, such as charitable donations, community projects, or partnerships with local organizations.

- Discuss how your clothing brand contributes positively to the communities it operates in.

4. Economic Impact

i.   Profitability and Growth:

- Provide financial data demonstrating the profitability and growth of your sustainable clothing brand.

- Highlight any financial benefits resulting from sustainability initiatives, such as cost savings or increased customer loyalty. (See Chapter 7)

ii.   Return on Sustainability Investment (ROSI):

- Calculate the return on investment for sustainability efforts, including energy-efficient equipment or sustainable sourcing practices.

- Show how sustainability initiatives contribute to the bottom line.

5. Future Goals and Commitments

- Outline your future sustainability goals and commitments, such as achieving carbon neutrality, expanding eco-friendly product lines, or increasing transparency.

- Describe the steps you plan to take to continually improve your brand's sustainability impact.

6. Conclusion

Summarize the key findings of your Sustainability Impact Assessment, emphasizing the positive contributions your sustainable clothing brand makes to the environment, society, and the economy.

7. Appendix (Optional)

Include any additional data, charts, or case studies that provide further evidence of your brand's sustainability impact.

By crafting a "Sustainability Impact Assessment" in this manner, your sustainable clothing brand can transparently communicate its commitment to sustainability, its achievements in reducing its environmental and social footprint, and its dedication to continual improvement. This assessment can also serve as a valuable tool for attracting environmentally and socially-conscious consumers and stakeholders.

8. Storytelling for Purpose

Master the art of purpose-driven storytelling. Learn how to translate your mission and values into narratives that connect with your audience on a deep emotional level. Use storytelling techniques like narrative arcs and metaphorical storytelling to convey your purpose effectively. Here's an example of using these techniques to craft a compelling mission statement:

Mission Statement: "The Beacon Collective"

Once upon a time, in a world brimming with challenges and opportunities, a group of visionary women came together. They were diverse in their backgrounds and experiences, but united by a shared purpose that burned brightly within their hearts.

As they embarked on their journey, they envisioned a lighthouse, standing tall amidst the tumultuous seas. This lighthouse, they knew, would not merely illuminate the path; it would be a symbol of hope, guidance, and unwavering support.

- The Call to Adventure: *Our story begins with a call to adventure—a beckoning to redefine the narrative of success. The Beacon Collective was born from a deep desire to inspire transformation, to challenge the status quo, and to lead with purpose.*

- The Heroine's Journey: *Like heroines of old tales, these women embarked on their journey, facing obstacles and self-discovery along the way. They knew that true leadership demanded integrity, inclusivity, and a commitment to excellence.*

- The Lighthouse of Change: *In the heart of their collective vision stood the lighthouse, a symbol of their mission. Just as a lighthouse guides ships safely to shore, The Beacon Collective guides individuals toward their fullest potential, ensuring no one is left adrift in the vast sea of possibilities.*

- The Climax: *Through innovation, inclusivity, and unyielding integrity, The Beacon Collective not only disrupted industries but also illuminated a path for others to follow. It became a beacon of empowerment, lighting the way for individuals to transform their lives.*

- The Resolution: *The journey continues, as The Beacon Collective remains committed to fostering inclusivity, driving innovation, and making a positive impact. Their purpose is to inspire transformation in the lives of their customers, and in doing so, create a world where every individual can thrive.*

As the sun sets on each day, The Beacon Collective's light shines brightly, a reminder of their unwavering commitment to their purpose. Their story is a testament to the power of unity, resilience, and a shared vision.

With The Beacon Collective, you are not merely engaging with a business; you are embarking on a journey of transformation, guided by a lighthouse of purpose that stands tall amidst the challenges and opportunities of our world.

This mission statement utilizes a narrative arc and metaphorical storytelling to convey the purpose of The Beacon Collective—a commitment to inspire transformation and be a guiding light in the lives of individuals. It paints a vivid picture of the business's journey, values, and the impact it aims to create, making the purpose not just a statement but a captivating story.

Section 2: Techniques for Overcoming Fear and Self-Doubt

Fear and self-doubt are common barriers that can obscure your passions and prevent you from pursuing your entrepreneurial dreams. In this section, I'll delve into techniques to help you conquer these inner obstacles and unleash your full potential.

1. Positive Affirmations

Positive affirmations are powerful statements that challenge and replace negative beliefs with positive ones. Positive affirmation techniques go beyond superficial repetition and focus on creating lasting change in your mindset:

- Specific Affirmations: Develop tailored affirmations that address your specific fears and doubts. For example, if you doubt your ability to succeed, create affirmations like, "I am fully capable of achieving my goals, and I have the skills and determination to do so."

- Visual Affirmations: Combine visual elements with affirmations to create a vision board or digital visualization that represents your desired outcomes. Visual affirmations tap into the power of imagery and reinforce your beliefs through daily exposure.

- Repetitive Practice: Incorporate positive affirmations into your daily routine. Repeatedly recite them in moments of self-doubt or incorporate them into meditation and mindfulness practices to reinforce your newfound beliefs.

2. Visualization

We will explore this more deeply in Chapter 3. Visualization is a technique that involves mentally imagining your desired outcomes. Visualization techniques take this practice to a higher level:

- Sensory-Rich Visualization: Engage all your senses while visualizing your success. Imagine not just the sights but also the sounds, smells, tastes, and tactile sensations associated with achieving your goals. This multisensory approach creates a more vivid and emotionally charged mental image.

- Future Pacing: In your visualization exercises, project yourself into the future and experience the success of your business firsthand. Feel the emotions, sense the surroundings, and visualize the positive impact your entrepreneurial journey will have on your life and the lives of others.

- Mental Rehearsal: Use visualization as a form of mental rehearsal. Imagine yourself confidently overcoming challenges and obstacles that have previously caused self-doubt. Mentally rehearse your actions and responses in situations where fear has held you back.

3. Cognitive Restructuring

Cognitive restructuring involves identifying and challenging negative thought patterns and replacing them with more constructive beliefs. Cognitive restructuring techniques help you reframe limiting beliefs:

- Socratic Questioning: Apply the Socratic method to your thoughts. When self-doubt arises, question it logically. Ask yourself probing questions like, "Is this belief based on evidence or assumptions?" and "What evidence suggests I can't succeed?"

- Mindfulness-Based Cognitive Restructuring: Combine mindfulness with cognitive restructuring to create awareness of your thoughts without judgment. When self-doubt surfaces, acknowledge it mindfully, then consciously choose to reframe it with a more positive and constructive belief.

- Affirmation Integration: Merge positive affirmations with cognitive restructuring. When you identify a negative thought, counter it with a corresponding positive affirmation. For instance, if you think, "I'm not qualified," respond with "I am constantly learning and growing, and my qualifications will continue to improve."

These techniques for overcoming fear and self-doubt can be transformative on your journey to discovering and pursuing your passions.

Chapter 3:
Igniting the Creative Spark

Welcome to the realm of innovation and creative thinking. In this chapter, I will explore techniques to awaken and harness your inner innovator. These strategies will not only fuel your entrepreneurial journey but also elevate your ability to generate groundbreaking ideas that can transform your business.

Section 1: The Power of Mindfulness—Cultivating the Creative Mind

In the fast-paced world of entrepreneurship, finding moments of calm and clarity can be a game-changer. The practice of mindfulness has a profound impact on creativity. Below we'll learn how to cultivate a heightened state of awareness, enabling you to observe your thoughts without judgment and tap into your creative inspiration.

Vipassana Meditation

Vipassana meditation is a mindfulness practice that originates from ancient Buddhist traditions. Its primary focus is on gaining insight into the true nature of reality and the self through self-observation and awareness. The word "Vipassana" means "insight" or "clear seeing" in Pali, the language of the original Buddhist texts.

Key Characteristics of Vipassana Meditation

- Focused Awareness: Vipassana meditation often starts with focused attention on the breath or bodily sensations to develop concentration.

- Observation: Practitioners are encouraged to observe their thoughts, feelings, bodily sensations, and mental processes without judgment. This observation is done with a sense of equanimity, neither clinging to nor resisting any experience.

- Insight: Through continued practice, meditators gain insight into the impermanent, ever-changing nature of all experiences, including the transient nature of physical sensations, emotions, and thoughts.

- Freedom from Suffering: The ultimate goal of Vipassana is to attain a deep understanding of the impermanence and interconnectedness of all things, which leads to liberation from suffering and the realization of one's true nature.

- Silent Retreats: Traditional Vipassana courses are often conducted in silent retreat settings, lasting for several days to allow practitioners to immerse themselves fully in the practice and deepen their insights.

- Non-Sectarian: Vipassana is non-sectarian and open to people of all backgrounds and beliefs. It is taught in a secular manner, focusing on the universal principles of mindfulness and insight.

Vipassana meditation is known for its rigorous and systematic approach to self-exploration, and it has gained popularity worldwide for its potential to bring about personal transformation and inner peace. It emphasizes the importance of direct experiential insight into the workings of the mind and the nature of reality as a path to profound personal growth and liberation from suffering.

Zen Meditation

Zen meditation, also known as Zazen, is a form of meditation rooted in Zen Buddhism. It is characterized by a focus on simplicity, mindfulness, and direct experience. Zen meditation aims to cultivate a deep understanding of the self and the nature of reality.

Key Characteristics of Zen Meditation

- Posture: Practitioners typically sit in a specific posture, often on a cushion (zafu) and a mat (zabuton) or directly on the floor. The back is kept straight, and the hands are positioned in a mudra, usually with the palms facing up and the fingers forming a particular shape.

- Breath Awareness: Attention is primarily directed toward the breath. Practitioners focus on the natural rhythm of their breathing, observing each inhalation and exhalation mindfully.

- Mindfulness: Zen meditation emphasizes mindfulness, which involves being fully present in the moment without judgment or attachment to thoughts, emotions, or sensations. Any thoughts that arise are acknowledged and allowed to pass without becoming distractions.

- Koans: In some Zen traditions, practitioners may work with koans—paradoxical questions or statements that are used as objects of meditation. Koans are intended to challenge the intellect and provoke insight beyond ordinary thinking.

- Silence: Zen meditation is often practiced in silence, with minimal guidance from instructors. This silence encourages practitioners to develop a direct, unmediated experience of reality.

- Teacher-Student Relationship: Zen often involves a close relationship between a teacher (Zen master) and student. The teacher provides guidance and may engage in one-on-one interviews (dokusan) to help students deepen their practice.

- Goalless Practice: Unlike some meditation practices that have specific goals, such as stress reduction or improved focus, Zen meditation is often seen as a goalless practice. The focus is on the process itself, rather than striving for specific outcomes.

- Enlightenment and Insight: The ultimate aim of Zen meditation is to gain insight into the true nature of reality and the self. This insight, often referred to as "enlightenment" or "kensho," is believed to bring profound clarity and freedom from suffering.

Zen meditation is renowned for its simplicity and directness. It encourages individuals to experience reality as it is, free from conceptualizations and mental constructs. Through sustained practice, Zen meditators seek to uncover deep insights into the nature of existence and awaken to a state of profound inner peace and wisdom.

Section 2: Visualization and Creative Visualization

Here we'll dive deeper in discovering how visualization exercises can stimulate your imagination and practically use the Socratic method to bring your business ideas to life. Visualization and Creative Visualization are powerful techniques for developing new business ideas by harnessing the power of imagination and mental imagery. Here's a short example of how these techniques can be applied:

Scenario: Starting a Sustainable Fashion Brand

1. Traditional Visualization

- Imagine yourself at the helm of a sustainable fashion brand. Picture the clothing line, envision the eco-friendly materials, and see the vibrant colors and innovative designs.

- Visualize a store filled with satisfied customers trying on your products, each piece representing your commitment to sustainability.

- See yourself collaborating with eco-conscious suppliers and passionate designers, all working together to create a positive impact on the fashion industry and the environment.

2. Creative Visualization

- Take traditional visualization a step further by engaging all your senses. Imagine the texture of sustainable fabrics, the smell of organic dyes, and the sound of a sewing machine crafting your designs.

- Create a vivid mental scenario where you're presenting your eco-friendly clothing line at a major fashion event, receiving accolades for your commitment to sustainability.

- Visualize how your brand's values align with your target audience's desires, creating a strong emotional connection with your customers.

3. Idea Generation

- After several sessions of visualization, you may find that your mind is teeming with new ideas. Perhaps you've envisioned innovative ways to source sustainable materials, unique marketing campaigns that resonate with your audience, or partnerships with like-minded organizations.

- One day, during your visualization practice, you might even see a breakthrough moment—a concept for a new, revolutionary product that perfectly aligns with your brand's mission.

4. Implementation

- With your newly generated ideas, you can start taking concrete steps toward launching your sustainable fashion brand. Your visualization sessions have not only sparked creativity but also instilled a strong sense of purpose and motivation.

- Your vision guides your decision-making process as you work toward bringing your ideas to life. You're driven by the mental image of a sustainable, successful business that leaves a positive mark on the fashion industry.

In this example, both traditional and creative visualization techniques are instrumental in shaping and nurturing the idea of starting a sustainable fashion brand. Visualization helps you access your creativity, visualize your goals, and align your actions with your envisioned future. By consistently practicing these techniques, you can develop and refine your business ideas, making them more vivid and achievable.

Section 3: The Curiosity-Driven Entrepreneur—Nurturing a Sense of Wonder

Curiosity is the spark that ignites innovation. In this part, I'll delve into the importance of curiosity and how it can serve as a powerful catalyst for creative thinking.

The Art of Asking Questions

Explore techniques for asking thought-provoking questions, such as the Socratic method. Learn how to question assumptions, challenge the status quo, and uncover unconventional solutions. Here's an example of how to use the Socratic method:

Innovation in Healthcare Services

Assumption: It's commonly assumed in the healthcare industry that patients need to physically visit a healthcare facility for most medical consultations and services.

Using the Socratic Method:

- Question 1: "Why is it assumed that physical visits are necessary for most medical consultations and services? What's the underlying rationale?"

  Response 1: "The assumption is based on the need for physical examinations, diagnostic tests, and in-person communication between doctors and patients."

- Question 2: "Are there technological advancements or alternative approaches that might challenge this assumption? How have telemedicine and remote monitoring been used in other healthcare contexts?"

Response 2: "Telemedicine and remote monitoring technologies have been used successfully in some cases, especially for routine check-ups and non-urgent consultations."

- Question 3: "What if we questioned the status quo and explored ways to expand our telemedicine and remote monitoring services? How might this impact patient accessibility and healthcare delivery?"

Response 3: "It could significantly improve accessibility, especially for patients in remote areas or with limited mobility. It might also reduce healthcare costs and waiting times for routine consultations."

- Question 4: "What are the potential challenges and opportunities in implementing and scaling up telemedicine and remote monitoring in our healthcare system?"

Response 4: "We'd need to invest in technology infrastructure, ensure data security and privacy, and train healthcare professionals. However, the opportunity to improve patient care and access is significant."

Outcome: By applying the Socratic method in the context of healthcare services, the healthcare team has initiated a discussion about unconventional solutions. They are now considering the broader use of telemedicine and remote monitoring to improve patient accessibility and healthcare delivery, challenging the traditional assumption that physical visits are always necessary. This exploration can lead to innovative improvements in healthcare services.

Section 4: Continuous Learning and Exploration

Here we will discover the concept of "lifelong learning" and how it can keep your mind agile and open to new ideas. I'll discuss learning strategies, such as meta-learning and the Feynman Technique, that can enhance your ability to absorb and apply knowledge.

Meta-Learning

Meta-learning is a learning strategy that involves learning how to learn. It's about understanding the processes, strategies, and methods that work best for you and adapting your learning approach accordingly. Here's a short example of how meta-learning applies to entrepreneurs:

Scenario: An Entrepreneur Starting a Tech Company

Meta-Learning in Action:

- Identifying Learning Styles: The entrepreneur realizes that they have a preference for visual learning. They process information better when they see diagrams, charts, and visual representations. They also recognize that they tend to learn best through practical, hands-on experience.

- Self-Assessment: Before diving into the tech industry, the entrepreneur takes time to assess their current knowledge and skills. They identify gaps in their understanding, such as a lack of coding skills, limited knowledge of software development, and little experience in managing a tech team.

- Learning Plan: Armed with self-awareness, the entrepreneur develops a learning plan. They decide to start by taking online coding courses that include visual aids and practical exercises. They also plan to attend tech meetups and network with experienced professionals in the industry to gain real-world insights.

- Adaptation: As they progress, the entrepreneur continuously assesses the effectiveness of their learning methods. They notice that the online courses are helpful, but they learn best when they work on small coding projects and collaborate with mentors. They adjust their learning plan accordingly.

- Iteration: The entrepreneur understands that learning is an ongoing process. They regularly revisit their learning goals, seek feedback from mentors, and adapt their strategies as they encounter new challenges and opportunities in the tech industry.

Outcome: By applying meta-learning principles, this maximizes your learning efficiency and effectiveness. You'll develop the skills and knowledge needed to succeed in the tech industry, all while continuously fine-tuning your learning approach. This meta-learning mindset allows you to navigate the ever-changing entrepreneurial landscape with adaptability and resilience.

The Feynman Technique

The Feynman Technique is a learning strategy named after the physicist Richard Feynman. It's a method for simplifying complex topics and enhancing understanding by teaching them to others in plain, everyday language. Here's a brief explanation of the Feynman Technique and how it can help entrepreneurs learn.

Steps:

- Choose a Topic: Select the topic or concept you want to learn or understand better. This could be a business strategy, a new technology, or any subject relevant to your entrepreneurial goals.

- Teach it Simply: Imagine you are teaching this topic to a complete beginner who has no prior knowledge of it. Use plain language and avoid jargon. Explain the concept step by step as if you were teaching a friend who knows nothing about it.

- Identify Gaps: As you explain the topic, pay attention to areas where your explanation becomes unclear or where you struggle to simplify it. These are the gaps in your understanding.

- Review and Refine: Go back to your study materials or resources and review the topic, paying special attention to the areas where you identified gaps in your understanding. Seek clarity and deeper comprehension.

How the Feynman Technique Helps Entrepreneurs

- Clarity of Understanding: By simplifying complex concepts into plain language, the Feynman Technique forces entrepreneurs to truly grasp the subject matter. This clear understanding is invaluable when making strategic decisions or communicating ideas to others.

- Identification of Knowledge Gaps: The technique highlights areas where your understanding may be incomplete or superficial. Entrepreneurs can then focus on filling these gaps to make more informed decisions.

- Effective Communication: Entrepreneurs often need to explain their business ideas and strategies to investors, team members, and customers. The Feynman Technique enhances the ability to communicate complex concepts in a way that others can easily grasp.

- Continuous Learning: In the ever-evolving business landscape, entrepreneurs must adapt and learn quickly. The Feynman Technique promotes ongoing learning and the development of a growth mindset, both of which are crucial for entrepreneurial success.

To summarize, the Feynman Technique is a powerful learning tool for entrepreneurs because it promotes deep understanding, helps identify knowledge gaps, improves communication skills, and encourages a mindset of continuous learning and adaptation, all of which are essential for success in the business world.

Section 5: The Observant Entrepreneur—Finding Inspiration in the Everyday

Observation is a skill that can transform ordinary experiences into extraordinary business ideas. In this section, I'll explore observational techniques to sharpen your powers of perception.

Observation Exercises:

The Art of Slow Observation

Practice techniques like slow-motion observation, where you meticulously study a situation, object, or process in slow motion to uncover hidden details and insights.

The Art of Slow Observation is a practice that involves taking the time to deeply observe and reflect on a situation, problem, or opportunity. It encourages entrepreneurs to step back, slow down, and gain valuable insights through careful observation. Here's a short example of how this practice can help entrepreneurs:

Scenario: A Startup Facing Stagnant Growth

The Art of Slow Observation in Action:

- Pause and Reflect: The entrepreneur notices that their startup's growth has plateaued. Instead of immediately diving into solutions, they decide to pause and reflect on the situation.

- Observation: They take time to observe various aspects of their business. They analyze customer feedback, market trends, and competitor strategies. They also pay attention to the company's internal dynamics, team morale, and operational processes.

- Ask Questions: During this observation period, the entrepreneur asks themselves questions like, "What are our customers saying about our product?" "Are there emerging trends we haven't noticed?" "Is there a bottleneck in our production process?" These questions guide their observation.

- Analyze Patterns: Through patient observation, the entrepreneur begins to identify patterns and connections. They notice that customer feedback consistently mentions a specific feature lacking in their product, and they also identify a recurring issue in the production process that's affecting quality.

- Innovative Solutions: Armed with these insights, the entrepreneur can now consider innovative solutions. They decide to prioritize the development of the missing product feature and implement process improvements in production.

Outcome: The Art of Slow Observation allows the entrepreneur to uncover the root causes of their business's stagnation. Instead of rushing into quick fixes, they take the time to truly understand the situation. This thoughtful observation leads to strategic decisions that address underlying issues and drive meaningful growth in their startup.

In this example, The Art of Slow Observation helps the entrepreneur make informed, strategic choices by first gaining a deep understanding of the challenges and opportunities in their business, ultimately leading to more effective decision-making and growth.

Empathetic Observation

Develop your ability to empathize deeply with others by observing their body language, facial expressions, and gestures. Here's an example of how empathy through observation can lead to customer-centric ideas:

Scenario: Launching a Data Analytics Platform for Enterprises

- Empathy Through Observation: Imagine an entrepreneur aiming to develop a data analytics platform tailored for large enterprises. To ensure the platform meets the unique needs of enterprise clients, they decide to deepen their understanding through observation.

- Observing Enterprise Challenges: The entrepreneur spends time at industry conferences and events, attending seminars and workshops on data analytics. They listen to presentations and engage with enterprise professionals.

- Body Language and Engagement: They observe the body language, engagement level, and expressions of the professionals during discussions about data analytics challenges. They take note of when topics generate enthusiasm or concern.

- Engaging in Conversations: The entrepreneur networks with enterprise executives and data analysts, asking questions like, "What are the main challenges your organization faces in harnessing data effectively?" and "What solutions have you tried, and what were the outcomes?"

Customer-Centric Insights

Through their observations and conversations, the entrepreneur gains deep insights into the needs and pain points of enterprise clients:

- They discover that enterprises are struggling with managing and analyzing large volumes of data efficiently, leading to information overload.

- They learn that data security and compliance are top priorities for enterprises, as data breaches can have severe consequences.

- They notice that many enterprises are eager to leverage analytics techniques like machine learning to gain a competitive edge.

Customer-Centric Business Ideas

Armed with these insights, the entrepreneur develops customer-centric business ideas for their data analytics platform:

- Scalable Data Management: They design the platform to handle vast amounts of data efficiently, offering scalable storage and processing capabilities to address the data overload challenge.

- Robust Security Measures: Recognizing the importance of data security, they implement state-of-the-art encryption and authentication features, ensuring compliance with industry regulations.

- Machine Learning Integration: They focus on integrating machine learning and AI algorithms into the platform, enabling enterprises to derive valuable insights and make data-driven decisions.

- Customizable Dashboards: To meet diverse needs, they offer customizable data visualization dashboards that allow users to tailor their analytics experience.

Outcome: By deeply empathizing with enterprise clients through observation, the entrepreneur develops a data analytics platform that directly addresses the complex challenges and priorities of large enterprises. This customer-centric approach not only attracts enterprise customers seeking powerful data analytics solutions but also positions the platform as a valuable tool for informed decision-making and competitive advantage.

Section 6: The Collaborative Entrepreneur—Fueling Innovation Through Diversity

Collaboration can be a wellspring of innovation. In this section, I'll explore how working with diverse individuals can ignite your creativity and yield unique business ideas.

Collaboration Strategies:

Cross-Disciplinary Collaboration

Delve into the world of cross-disciplinary collaboration. Learn how to partner with experts from different fields to gain fresh perspectives and novel solutions.

Here's a short example of how cross-disciplinary collaboration can help you:

Scenario: Launching an Innovative Health-Tech Startup

Cross-Disciplinary Collaboration in Action:

Imagine an entrepreneur who wants to create an innovative health-tech startup focused on improving remote patient monitoring. They recognize that achieving this goal requires expertise from multiple disciplines.

- Healthcare Experts: The entrepreneur collaborates with healthcare professionals, including doctors, nurses, and medical researchers. They bring in their deep knowledge of patient needs, medical protocols, and data security in healthcare.

- Tech Specialists: Recognizing the technological challenges, the entrepreneur partners with software engineers and data scientists. These experts can design and develop the remote monitoring software, ensuring it's user-friendly and secure.

- Designers and User Experience (UX) Experts: To create an intuitive and patient-friendly interface, the entrepreneur involves designers and UX experts. Their input ensures that the platform is easy to navigate and engaging for patients.

- Regulatory and Compliance Consultants: Given the stringent regulations in healthcare, the entrepreneur collaborates with regulatory consultants who specialize in healthcare compliance. They help navigate legal requirements and ensure the platform meets industry standards.

- Business Strategists: To create a viable business model, the entrepreneur works with business strategists and financial experts who can analyze market trends, assess competition, and develop a sustainable revenue strategy.

Benefits of Cross-Disciplinary Collaboration

- Innovation: By bringing together experts from various fields, the entrepreneur can leverage diverse perspectives and innovative ideas to create a unique and effective remote monitoring solution.

- Comprehensive Solution: Cross-disciplinary collabo-ration ensures that the startup addresses all aspects of the healthcare technology, from medical accuracy to user experience and compliance, resulting in a comprehensive solution.

- Market Understanding: Collaboration with business strategists helps the entrepreneur gain a deep understanding of the market, ensuring that the startup's product aligns with customer needs and market demands.

- Reduced Risks: Collaboration with regulatory consultants minimizes legal and compliance risks, ensuring that the startup operates within the bounds of healthcare regulations.

Outcome: Through cross-disciplinary collaboration, you can develop a cutting-edge health-tech solution that not only meets the highest medical standards but is also user-friendly, compliant with regulations, and strategically positioned in the market. This collaborative approach increases the chances of success for the startup in the competitive healthcare technology sector.

Section 7: Creative Problem-Solving Teams

Explore techniques for assembling and leading creative problem-solving teams. I'll discuss strategies like brainstorming marathons and the Six Thinking Hats method.

Brainstorming Marathons

Here's a short example of how brainstorming marathons can help entrepreneurs:

Scenario: Developing a New Mobile App for Travel Enthusiasts

Brainstorming Marathon in Action:

Imagine an entrepreneur who is passionate about travel and wants to create a mobile app that provides unique travel experiences to users. They decide to organize a brainstorming marathon with their team to generate creative ideas for the app.

- Preparation: The entrepreneur gathers a diverse team of individuals with various backgrounds and skills, including travel enthusiasts, app developers, designers, and marketing experts. They set up a comfortable and collaborative workspace with whiteboards, sticky notes, and markers.

- Time-Bound Session: The brainstorming marathon is a dedicated, time-bound session lasting several hours or even a full day. The team is encouraged to suspend judgment and generate as many ideas as possible.

- Idea Generation: During the marathon, team members start sharing ideas related to the travel app. They explore features, user interfaces, and unique value propositions. Some ideas might involve gamification, personalized itineraries, or community-building features.

- Combining and Refining: As ideas flow, the team begins to build on each other's concepts. They combine and refine ideas to create more comprehensive and innovative solutions. For instance, they might merge the concept of personalized itineraries with a social platform for travelers to share experiences.

- Prioritization: Towards the end of the marathon, the team reviews and prioritizes the generated ideas based on feasibility, market potential, and alignment with the app's core mission.

Benefits of Brainstorming Marathon

- Diverse Perspectives: The marathon involves team members with different backgrounds and experiences, leading to a wider range of ideas and perspectives.

- Quantity of Ideas: The time-bound and collaborative nature of the marathon encourages participants to generate a large number of ideas, increasing the chances of uncovering unique and innovative concepts.

- Combination of Ideas: By building on each other's ideas, the team can create more comprehensive and integrated solutions that may not have emerged through individual brainstorming.

- Efficient Idea Prioritization: The marathon provides a structured environment for quickly assessing and prioritizing ideas, ensuring that the most promising ones are pursued.

Outcome: The brainstorming marathon results in a pool of creative and well-considered ideas for the travel app. The entrepreneur and their team can then take these ideas, refine them further, and ultimately develop a mobile app that stands out in the competitive travel industry, offering unique and exciting experiences to users.

The Six Thinking Hats Method

Additionally, the Six Thinking Hats method can also help entrepreneurs explore new business ideas:

Scenario: Developing a Sustainable Packaging Solution for E-commerce Businesses

Imagine an entrepreneur who is passionate about sustainability and wants to create a business that offers eco-friendly packaging solutions for e-commerce companies. They gather a team to brainstorm and use the Six Thinking Hats method to explore various aspects of their business idea.

- White Hat (Facts and Information): The team starts by wearing the White Hat, focusing on gathering facts and information. They research current packaging materials, environmental impact statistics, and industry trends related to sustainable packaging.

- Red Hat (Emotions and Feelings): Next, they switch to the Red Hat, where team members express their emotions and gut feelings about the idea. Some express enthusiasm for promoting sustainability, while others voice concerns about the cost implications of eco-friendly materials.

- Yellow Hat (Positive Thinking): Wearing the Yellow Hat, the team focuses on positive aspects of the idea. They identify potential benefits like attracting eco-conscious customers, gaining a competitive edge, and contributing to a greener planet.

- Black Hat (Critical Thinking): Now, they put on the Black Hat and examine potential drawbacks and risks. They discuss challenges such as the initial cost of sustainable materials, the need for education around eco-friendly packaging, and market competition.

- Green Hat (Creative Thinking): Transitioning to the Green Hat, the team engages in creative thinking to generate innovative ideas. They brainstorm ways to reduce the cost of sustainable materials, develop unique packaging designs, and collaborate with e-commerce companies for mutual benefit.

- Blue Hat (Process Control): Finally, they don the Blue Hat to manage the thinking process. They discuss action steps, prioritize ideas, and outline a plan for further research and development.

Benefits of the Six Thinking Hats Method

- Structured Exploration: The method provides a structured framework for exploring different aspects of the business idea, ensuring that both positive and negative considerations are thoroughly examined.

- Holistic Perspective: By wearing different "hats," team members can approach the idea from various angles, promoting a holistic understanding of its potential.

- Creativity: The Green Hat encourages creative thinking, helping the team generate innovative solutions and ideas.

- Effective Decision-Making: The Blue Hat ensures that the brainstorming session leads to actionable next steps and decisions.

Outcome: Using the Six Thinking Hats method, the entrepreneur and their team gain a comprehensive understanding of the sustainable packaging business idea. They identify potential challenges and risks while also generating creative solutions and strategies for success. This well-rounded exploration guides them in making informed decisions as they move forward with their eco-friendly packaging venture.

Chapter 4:
Market Mastery

Section 1: Know Your Audience

Understanding your target audience is the compass that guides your business decisions. It's not just about identifying demographics; it's about gaining a deep, empathetic understanding of your ideal customers. In this chapter, I will explore techniques for getting inside the minds of your audience, uncovering their pain points, desires, and preferences to tailor your product or service effectively.

Building Comprehensive Customer Personas

Creating customer personas goes beyond a superficial understanding of your audience. It involves developing detailed and nuanced profiles of your ideal customers. Here's how to do it effectively:

1. Demographic Analysis: While basic demographics like age, gender, and location are important, delve deeper into demographic factors:

- Behavioral Demographics: Analyze your audience's behaviors, such as online habits, purchasing patterns, and lifestyle choices. This data can reveal valuable insights into their decision-making processes.

- Psychographic Profiling: Explore your audience's values, beliefs, and psychographic characteristics. What motivates them? What are their core values? Understanding these aspects can help you connect with them on a deeper level.

2. Pain Point Identification: In-depth interviews and surveys are powerful tools for identifying pain points your audience faces. Techniques include:

- Laddering Technique: Use this interviewing technique to uncover the underlying motivations behind your customers' pain points. Ask "why" repeatedly to get to the root cause of their challenges.

- Emotion-Centric Surveys: Craft surveys that focus on the emotional aspects of your audience's experiences. Ask them to describe how specific problems make them feel. Emotions often drive purchasing decisions. I use SurveyMonkey—it's great and easy to use.

3. Persona Scenario Mapping: Go beyond static personas by creating dynamic persona scenarios. Imagine your personas' daily lives, their challenges, and how your product or service fits into their routines. This technique helps you see your business from their perspective.

Conducting Customer Interviews

Interviews are a treasure trove of insights when done right. Interviewing techniques can extract richer information from your audience:

1. Ethnographic Interviews: Immerse yourself in your customers' environments. Observe their behaviors and routines firsthand. Ethnographic interviews help you understand the context in which your product or service fits into their lives.

2. Longitudinal Interviews: Conduct interviews over an extended period to track changes in your customers' needs and preferences. This approach ensures that your business remains aligned with their evolving expectations.

3. Empathy-Driven Interviews: Develop deep empathy for your customers by actively listening and validating their experiences. Empathetic interviewing creates a safe space for customers to share their thoughts, fears, and aspirations openly.

Using Survey Techniques

Surveys are valuable tools for collecting data at scale. Survey techniques go beyond basic questions and employ strategies such as:

1. Conjoint Analysis: Conjoint analysis helps you understand how customers prioritize features or attributes in your product or service. By presenting them with various product configurations, you can pinpoint their preferences with precision.

2. MaxDiff Analysis: MaxDiff, or maximum difference scaling, helps you determine the relative importance of different features or attributes. It's a valuable technique for fine-tuning product development.

3. Sentiment Analysis: Leverage natural language processing and sentiment analysis tools to analyze open-ended survey responses. This technique uncovers trends and emotions in customer feedback.

Section 2: Keeping Tabs on the Competition

To thrive, you need to know your competition inside and out. Here I'll teach you the art of competitor analysis, helping you identify strengths, weaknesses, and opportunities. This insight will help you craft a unique selling proposition (USP) that sets your business apart.

Why Competitor Analysis Matters

Before I delve into the techniques, let's understand why competitor analysis is essential for your business:

1. Strategic Insights: Competitor analysis provides strategic insights into the competitive landscape. It helps you identify emerging trends, market shifts, and gaps in the market that you can exploit.

2. Identifying Strengths and Weaknesses: By studying your competitors, you can uncover their strengths and weaknesses. This knowledge allows you to leverage your own strengths and exploit their vulnerabilities.

3. Innovation and Improvement: Competitor analysis can inspire innovation and improvement. By understanding what your competitors do, you can challenge your team to exceed those standards.

4. Risk Mitigation: It helps you anticipate competitive threats and develop contingency plans. Knowing your competition prepares you to react swiftly to changes in the market.

Techniques for Competitor Analysis

Now, let's explore techniques for conducting comprehensive competitor analysis:

1. In-Depth SWOT Analysis: While a traditional SWOT analysis (Strengths, Weaknesses, Opportunities, Threats) is valuable, an approach involves:

- Cross-Referencing: Compare your SWOT analysis with that of your competitors. This cross-referencing reveals areas where you can differentiate yourself or capitalize on their weaknesses.

- Scenario Analysis: Use the SWOT analysis to develop various scenarios for your business's future. These scenarios help you prepare for different competitive landscapes.

2. Customer Perception Mapping: Gain insight into how customers perceive your competitors. Techniques include:

- Customer Surveys: Conduct surveys to gauge customer perceptions of your competitors' products, services, and brands. Analyze the data to identify areas for improvement or differentiation.

- Sentiment Analysis: Use natural language processing and sentiment analysis to mine online reviews and social media conversations related to your competitors. This technique reveals not only what customers say but also how they feel.

3. Benchmarking: Benchmarking goes beyond comparing basic metrics. It involves:

- Process Benchmarking: Analyze your competitors' internal processes, from supply chain management to customer service. Identify areas where you can optimize and streamline your operations.

- Best Practice Adoption: Study your competition's best practices and consider adopting them, or adapting them to suit your unique business model.

4. Competitive Intelligence Gathering: Explore competitive intelligence techniques, such as:

- Deep IAB Analysis: Go beyond surface-level research by delving into the deep IAB, where less accessible information resides. IAB scraping tools and data analytics can uncover hidden competitive insights. This analysis involves studying the industry's structure, competitive landscape, market trends, key players, regulations, and other critical factors that influence its performance.

- The goal of deep IAB analysis is to help businesses, entrepreneurs, and investors make informed decisions by providing a thorough understanding of the industry in question. It goes beyond surface-level research and dives deep into the nuances and dynamics that shape the industry's present and future.

- This type of analysis is essential for assessing market opportunities, understanding competitive forces, identifying potential risks, and formulating effective business strategies tailored to the specific industry's conditions. Ultimately, deep IAB analysis serves as a valuable tool for strategic planning and decision-making within a particular sector.

- Competitor Interviews: Conduct discreet interviews with former employees or industry insiders to gain insider knowledge about your competitors' strategies and weaknesses.

5. Scenario Planning: Develop scenario planning techniques to anticipate various competitive scenarios. These scenarios can inform your strategic decisions and risk mitigation strategies. Here's how:

    i.   Start with a Solid Foundation

- Gather Data: Begin by collecting relevant data on your industry, competitors, and market trends. The more data you have, the more accurate your scenarios can be.

- Understand Your Business: Have a deep understanding of your own business, its strengths, weaknesses, opportunities, and threats (SWOT analysis).

    ii.   Identify Key Variables

- Critical Factors: Determine the key variables or drivers that significantly impact your business. These could include market demand, pricing, technology, regulatory changes, and consumer behavior.

iii.   Create Multiple Scenarios

- Best-Case Scenario: Develop a scenario where everything goes exceptionally well for your business. Consider factors like rapid growth, high demand, and minimal competition.

- Worst-Case Scenario: Create a scenario where things take a turn for the worse. Think about challenges such as economic downturns, supply chain disruptions, or increased competition.

- Most Likely Scenario: Develop a scenario that represents the most probable outcome based on current trends and data.

- Wildcard Scenarios: Consider unexpected events or disruptions that could have a major impact on your business. These could be natural disasters, political changes, or technological breakthroughs.

iv.   Assess Impact and Likelihood

- Rate Scenarios: Assign a likelihood and impact rating to each scenario. This helps you prioritize your focus.

- Probability Analysis: Use statistical methods to estimate the probability of each scenario occurring based on historical data and trends.

v.   Develop Strategies for Each Scenario

- Action Plans: Create specific strategies and action plans for each scenario. Determine how you would respond, adapt, or pivot your business in each situation.

- Resource Allocation: Decide how you would allocate resources (financial, human, and technological) in each scenario.

vi. Regularly Review and Update

- Dynamic Process: Scenario planning is not a one-time exercise. Regularly review and update your scenarios as market conditions and variables change.

- Feedback Loop: Seek input from employees, advisors, and industry experts to ensure your scenarios are well-informed.

vii. Stress Testing

- Test Resilience: Conduct stress tests to assess how well your business can withstand extreme scenarios. This involves examining your financial stability, supply chain resilience, and operational flexibility.

viii. Monitor Early Warning Signals

- Identify Indicators: Establish a system for monitoring early warning signals that may indicate a shift towards one of your scenarios.

- Stay Informed: Keep yourself updated on industry news, market trends, and global events that could trigger a scenario.

ix. Decision-Making Framework

- Use as a Guide: Scenario planning should serve as a guide for decision-making rather than a rigid prediction. When real-world conditions change, refer to your scenarios to inform your choices.

Scenario planning helps you become more proactive in responding to changes and challenges in the competitive landscape. It allows you to develop a flexible and adaptable business strategy that can thrive in various conditions, ensuring your long-term success as an entrepreneur.

Chapter 5:
Crafting Your Success Blueprint

Crafting a success blueprint empowers new entrepreneurs by providing you with a structured plan, fostering clarity and focus, and enabling you to make informed decisions. It is a crucial tool for navigating the challenging journey of starting and growing a business. Crafting a success blueprint can significantly help new entrepreneurs for several reasons:

- Clarity and Direction: A success blueprint forces you to define your vision, mission, and goals clearly. This clarity provides a sense of direction and purpose, ensuring that your efforts are aligned with your ultimate objectives.

- Prioritization: It helps entrepreneurs prioritize tasks and allocate resources effectively. By setting specific goals and timelines, you can focus on what matters most and avoid getting sidetracked by less critical activities.

- Risk Mitigation: A well-thought-out blueprint includes market research and risk assessments. This enables entrepreneurs to identify potential challenges and develop strategies to mitigate them, reducing the likelihood of costly setbacks.

- Resource Management: Entrepreneurs often have limited resources, especially in the early stages. A blueprint helps them allocate their resources—financial, time, and manpower—efficiently and avoid wastage.

- Flexibility: While providing a structured plan, a success blueprint remains adaptable. It allows you to revise your strategies in response to changing market conditions, new opportunities, or unexpected obstacles.

- Motivation and Accountability: Having a blueprint in place can serve as a source of motivation. As an entrepreneur, you can track your progress against the goals you've set, which can boost morale and hold you accountable for taking action.

- Communication: A success blueprint can also be a valuable communication tool when seeking support from investors, partners, or team members. It clearly conveys the business's vision, strategy, and growth potential.

The Power of Clarity

In the world of entrepreneurship, clarity is your compass. A clear vision and well-defined goals serve as the guiding stars that lead your business to success. In this chapter, I will delve into the art of defining your mission and vision effectively and harnessing the magic of setting SMART goals—Specific, Measurable, Achievable, Relevant, and Time-bound. By the end of this section, you'll have the tools to create a concise, one-page business plan that crystallizes your path forward.

Setting SMART Goals:

1. Specific Goals

In goal-setting, specificity is key. Clearly define your objectives, leaving no room for ambiguity. Consider using techniques like the "5 Whys" to dig deeper and identify the underlying reasons for your goals.

The "5 Whys" is a problem-solving technique that helps new entrepreneurs identify the root causes of issues or challenges within their business. It involves asking "why" repeatedly to drill down into the underlying causes of a problem. By doing so, you can uncover the true source of the issue and develop effective solutions. Here's how it works:

- Identify the Problem: Start by clearly defining the problem or challenge you're facing in your business. It could be a decrease in sales, customer complaints, operational inefficiencies, or any other issue.

- Ask "Why" Once: Begin by asking why the problem occurred. For example, if your sales have decreased, you might ask, "Why did our sales drop?"

- Repeat "Why" Four More Times: After the first "why" question, continue to ask "why" in response to the previous answer. Each subsequent "why" should aim to dig deeper into the causes. For example:

i. First "Why": Our sales dropped because customer demand decreased.

ii. Second "Why": Why did customer demand decrease? Because our marketing efforts weren't effective.

iii. Third "Why": Why weren't our marketing efforts effective? Because we didn't target the right audience.

iv. Fourth "Why": Why didn't we target the right audience? Because we didn't conduct thorough market research.

v. Fifth "Why": Why didn't we conduct thorough market research? Because we lacked the necessary market data and analysis.

- Reach the Root Cause: Continue asking "why" until you reach a point where the answer identifies the fundamental or root cause of the problem. In the example above, the root cause is the lack of market data and analysis.

- Develop Solutions: Once you've identified the root cause, you can start brainstorming and implementing solutions to address it. In this case, the solution would involve conducting comprehensive market research to better understand your target audience.

The "5 Whys" technique helps entrepreneurs avoid addressing only the symptoms of a problem and instead get to the core issues that need to be resolved. It encourages a more thorough and systematic approach to problem-solving, leading to more effective and sustainable solutions.

Remember that while asking "why" five times is a guideline, the actual number of iterations may vary depending on the complexity of the issue. The key is to keep asking "why" until you are confident that you have identified the root cause and can take meaningful action to address it.

2. Measurable Goals

Measurement techniques involve setting specific metrics and key performance indicators (KPIs) to track your progress. Utilize data analytics and tracking tools to monitor and evaluate your performance accurately.

Setting Key Performance Indicators (KPIs) is a crucial step for new entrepreneurs, and utilizing data analytics and tracking tools can greatly enhance your ability to monitor and evaluate your performance accurately. Here's how you can do it:

- Define Clear KPIs

Start by defining specific, measurable, and relevant KPIs that align with your business goals. Examples could include sales revenue, customer acquisition cost, website traffic, conversion rate, or customer satisfaction scores.

- Select the Right Tools

Choose data analytics and tracking tools that best suit your needs and budget. Popular options include Google Analytics, social media analytics platforms, email marketing analytics, and customer relationship management (CRM) software.

- Implement Tracking Codes

If using online platforms like a website or e-commerce store, implement tracking codes and pixels to collect data. These codes help capture user interactions and behaviors on your online assets.

- Integrate Data Sources

Integrate data sources whenever possible. For instance, connect your website analytics with your CRM system to track the customer journey from acquisition to conversion.

- Set Up Dashboards

Create customized dashboards within your analytics tools to display your KPIs in real-time. Dashboards provide a quick overview of your performance and allow you to spot trends and anomalies.

- Regularly Review Data

Schedule regular reviews of your data, ideally on a weekly or monthly basis. Look for patterns, changes, and outliers in your KPIs.

- Utilize Analytics

Explore analytics features within your tools, such as cohort analysis, funnel visualization, and attribution modeling. These features can provide deeper insights into customer behavior and conversion paths.

- Segment Your Data

Segment your data to gain a better understanding of different customer groups or marketing channels. Segmentation can reveal opportunities for optimization and targeting.

- A/B Testing and Experimentation

Implement A/B tests and experiments to optimize various aspects of your business, such as website design, marketing campaigns, or product offerings. Analyze the results to make data-driven decisions.

- Data Visualization

Use data visualization tools to create graphs, charts, and reports that make complex data more understandable. Visualizations can help you communicate insights to your team or stakeholders effectively.

- Continuous Improvement

Continuously monitor your KPIs and use the insights gained to refine your strategies and tactics. Make data-driven adjustments to your business plan as needed.

- Training and Skill Development

Invest in training or hire professionals who specialize in data analytics and interpretation to ensure you're making the most of your data.

- Data Privacy and Security

Ensure that you comply with data privacy regulations and implement security measures to protect sensitive customer data.

By following these steps and leveraging data analytics and tracking tools effectively, new entrepreneurs can gain valuable insights into their business's performance, identify areas for improvement, and make informed decisions that drive growth and success.

3. Achievable Goals

Achievability assessment involves a comprehensive analysis of resources, capabilities, and potential obstacles. Employ techniques like a resource audit to ensure you have what it takes to achieve your goals.

Conducting a resource audit is a valuable process for new entrepreneurs to assess whether they have the necessary resources to achieve their business goals. Here's how to employ this technique effectively:

- Define Your Goals

Start by clearly defining your business goals and objectives. Whether it's increasing sales, expanding into new markets, or launching a new product, your goals should be specific, measurable, achievable, relevant, and time-bound (SMART).

- Identify Required Resources

Determine the resources required to accomplish your goals. These resources can include financial capital, physical assets (e.g., equipment or facilities), human resources (e.g., skilled employees), technology, and intellectual property.

- Create a Resource Inventory

List all the resources currently available to your business. This includes both tangible assets (like cash, inventory, and equipment) and intangible assets (such as patents, trademarks, and intellectual capital).

- Assess Resource Adequacy

Evaluate whether your existing resources are sufficient to support your goals. Consider factors like quantity, quality, and accessibility. Are there any resource gaps or limitations that could hinder your progress?

- Prioritize Resources

Prioritize your resources based on their importance and relevance to your goals. Some resources may be critical, while others may be secondary. Allocate your resources accordingly.

- Identify Resource Constraints

Determine if there are any resource constraints that need to be addressed. For example, if you lack the necessary funds, you may need to explore financing options. If you need specific skills, you might consider hiring or partnering with experts.

- Explore Resource Optimization

Look for ways to optimize the use of your existing resources. This can involve improving resource efficiency, reducing waste, or reallocating resources to higher-priority tasks.

- Resource Acquisition

If you identify resource gaps that cannot be addressed internally, explore options for acquiring additional resources. This might involve securing funding through investors, loans, or grants or hiring new team members with the required skills.

- Risk Assessment

Consider the risks associated with resource availability. What if a key resource becomes unavailable or more expensive? Develop contingency plans to mitigate potential risks.

- Regular Monitoring

Resource audits should not be a one-time activity. Regularly monitor your resources and their alignment with your goals, especially as your business evolves. Make adjustments as needed.

- Seek Expert Advice

If you're unsure about resource allocation or acquisition, don't hesitate to seek advice from mentors, industry experts, or business consultants who can provide guidance based on their experience.

- Document Your Resource Strategy

Create a resource strategy that outlines your resource allocation plan, how you'll address resource constraints, and your approach to resource optimization. This document can serve as a valuable reference.

By conducting a resource audit and effectively managing your resources, you can ensure that you have the necessary assets and capabilities to pursue your business goals with confidence. It helps you make informed decisions, allocate resources wisely, and enhance your chances of success as a new entrepreneur.

4. Relevant Goals

Relevance assessment requires aligning your goals with your mission and vision. Ensure that each goal contributes meaningfully to your overall business objectives. Here's how to do it effectively:

- Understand Your Mission and Vision

Start by revisiting and understanding your mission and vision statements. Your mission statement defines the purpose of your business, while your vision statement outlines the long-term goals and aspirations.

- Identify Your Core Values

Determine the core values that guide your business. These values should reflect the principles and beliefs that are fundamental to your mission and vision.

- Establish Clear Business Goals

Define specific and measurable business goals that are aligned with your mission and vision. These goals should represent what you want to achieve in the short term while moving closer to your long-term vision.

- Prioritize Your Goals

Prioritize your goals based on their alignment with your mission and vision. Some goals will be more directly related to your core purpose, while others may serve as stepping stones toward your broader vision.

- Evaluate Relevance

Assess each goal's relevance to your mission and vision. Ask yourself how achieving a particular goal contributes to fulfilling your mission and bringing you closer to realizing your vision.

- Create an Action Plan

Develop a detailed action plan for each goal. Outline the specific steps, resources, and timelines needed to achieve them. Ensure that each action plan aligns with your overall mission and vision.

- Measure Progress

Implement key performance indicators (KPIs) to measure your progress toward each goal. These KPIs should reflect the impact of your actions on your mission and vision.

- Regularly Review and Adjust

Periodically review your goals, action plans, and progress. Be open to adjustments and refinements as your business evolves.

Goals that are no longer relevant to your mission or vision may need to be revised or replaced.

- Communicate Your Alignment

Share your aligned goals, mission, and vision with your team, stakeholders, and customers. This helps create a shared sense of purpose and commitment.

- Stay True to Your Values

Throughout your journey, ensure that your actions and decisions align with your core values, as these are the foundation of your mission and vision.

- Celebrate Milestones

Celebrate achievements and milestones that bring you closer to your mission and vision. Recognize and reward the efforts that contribute to your overall objectives.

- Stay Focused and Adaptable

While it's important to align your goals with your mission and vision, also remain adaptable. Business environments can change, and you may need to adjust your goals to stay on course.

- Seek Feedback

Encourage feedback from team members, mentors, and advisors. They can provide valuable insights into how well your goals align with your mission and vision.

By aligning your goals with your mission and vision, you create a clear path for your business's growth and development. This alignment ensures that every step you take brings you closer to realizing your broader vision while staying true to the core values that define your business.

5. Time-Bound Goals

In time-bound goal setting, create a detailed timeline with milestones and deadlines. Consider employing project management methodologies like Agile or Scrum to manage your goals effectively.

Here's how to do it, including considerations for employing project management methodologies like Agile or Scrum:

Creating a Detailed Timeline

- Define Your Goals

Start by clearly defining your business goals. These goals should be specific, measurable, achievable, relevant, and time-bound (SMART).

- Break Down Goals into Milestones

Divide each goal into smaller, manageable milestones. Milestones are key progress points that help you track your journey toward the goal.

- Assign Deadlines

Assign specific deadlines to each milestone. These deadlines should be realistic and based on your overall goal's timeframe.

- Use a Visual Timeline

Create a visual timeline or project plan that outlines all your milestones and deadlines. Tools like Gantt charts or project management software can be highly effective for this purpose.

- Identify Dependencies

Recognize any dependencies between milestones. Some milestones may need to be completed before others can begin.

- Allocate Resources

Ensure that you have the necessary resources, including personnel, budget, and equipment, allocated for each milestone.

- Regularly Review and Adjust

Periodically review your timeline and assess your progress. If you find that you're falling behind or that circumstances have changed, be prepared to adjust your deadlines accordingly.

- Prioritize Tasks

Within each milestone, prioritize tasks based on their importance and urgency. This helps you focus on what needs to be done first.

- Communicate and Collaborate

If you're working with a team, maintain open communication and collaboration. Ensure that everyone understands their roles and responsibilities within the timeline.

Consider Employing Agile or Scrum

Agile and Scrum are project management methodologies that are highly adaptable and can be particularly useful for new entrepreneurs. Here's how you can consider using them:

- Agile Methodology

Agile focuses on iterative development and customer collaboration. It allows you to break larger goals into smaller "sprints," typically lasting two to four weeks. Each sprint results in a potentially shippable product or deliverable.

- Scrum Framework

Scrum is a subset of Agile and provides a structured framework for project management. It involves daily stand-up meetings, backlog grooming, sprint planning, and sprint reviews. Scrum can help you manage your goals with a strong emphasis on teamwork and adaptability.

- Benefits of Agile/Scrum

These methodologies encourage flexibility, adaptability, and responsiveness to changing circumstances. They also prioritize customer feedback and continuous improvement.

- Training and Resources

If you're interested in using Agile or Scrum, consider investing in training or resources to understand the methodologies better. Many online courses and certifications are available.

- Start Small

If you're new to Agile or Scrum, start with small projects or goals to gain familiarity and experience with the methodologies.

By creating a detailed timeline and considering project management methodologies like Agile or Scrum, you can effectively manage your goals, stay organized, and adapt to changes, ultimately increasing your chances of success as a new entrepreneur.

6. Crafting Your One-Page Business Plan:

Synthesize your mission, vision, and SMART goals into a one-page business plan. This concise document serves as a constant reminder of your purpose and objectives.

Here's an example of a one-page business plan for a fictional handcrafted jewelry business. (Again, feel free to use this as a template for creating yours—it's what it's here for!)

Business Name: The Artisan Jewel Box

Mission Statement: To create exquisite handcrafted jewelry that celebrates individuality and craftsmanship, making artisanal pieces accessible to jewelry enthusiasts worldwide.

Vision Statement: To be the preferred choice for those seeking unique, high-quality jewelry that tells a story, inspires confidence, and connects people to the artistry behind each piece.

SMART Goals:

- Specific: Launch The Artisan Jewel Box's e-commerce website by (Date: Six Months from Today).

- Measurable: Achieve (Number: First-Year Sales) in the first year, with a focus on online sales growth.

- Achievable: Secure partnerships with (Number: Local Boutiques) for in-store displays within the first year.

- Relevant: Build a strong social media presence with (Number: X) Instagram followers and (Number: X) Facebook likes within (Timeframe: One Year).

- Time-bound: Open our first physical store in (Location: City) by (Date: End of Year Two), expanding our reach and visibility.

This one-page business plan concisely encapsulates the essence of The Artisan Jewel Box. It outlines the mission and vision statements, providing a clear sense of purpose and direction. Additionally, SMART goals are established to guide the business's growth and development over a defined timeframe. This document serves as a constant reminder of the business's objectives and acts as a reference point for strategic decision-making.

Chapter 6:
Building Your Brand and
Navigating Marketing Magic

Building Your Brand and Navigating Marketing Magic are essential for new entrepreneurs because they help define the business's identity, attract and retain customers, generate awareness, maintain consistency, expand reach, adapt to changes, and measure the effectiveness of marketing efforts. These elements are critical for the success and growth of any new venture. Let me explain further:

1. Establishing Identity and Trust: Building a strong brand helps entrepreneurs create a unique identity for their business. It's about more than just a logo; it encompasses the values, mission, and personality of the brand. A well-defined brand can instill trust and credibility in customers and differentiate the business in a competitive market.

2. Attracting and Retaining Customers: Effective branding and marketing strategies attract the right audience by resonating with their needs and preferences. Entrepreneurs who navigate marketing magic understand how to communicate their brand's value proposition effectively, ensuring that potential customers become loyal ones.

3. Generating Awareness: In a noisy marketplace, branding and marketing efforts are essential for getting noticed. A well-crafted brand and marketing strategy increase the visibility of the business, making it easier for customers to find and engage with the products or services offered.

4. Building Consistency: Consistency in branding and marketing efforts helps establish a strong brand presence. Entrepreneurs who navigate marketing magic understand the importance of maintaining a consistent brand image and messaging across all channels, from social media to packaging.

5. Expanding Reach: Effective marketing strategies, including digital marketing and social media, enable entrepreneurs to reach a broader audience. Navigating marketing magic involves understanding which platforms and tactics will resonate most with the target market and how to leverage them effectively.

6. Adapting to Changes: The world of marketing is ever-evolving, with new technologies and trends constantly emerging. Entrepreneurs who navigate marketing magic stay agile and adapt their strategies to align with changing consumer behavior and preferences.

7. Measuring ROI: Entrepreneurs should not only invest in marketing but also understand the return on that investment. Navigating marketing magic involves setting measurable goals and tracking key performance indicators to ensure that marketing efforts are delivering results.

Section 1: Crafting Your Brand Identity

Your brand is your promise to your customers. I'll explore the art of storytelling, teaching you how to share your unique journey authentically. I'll delve into branding essentials like creating a memorable logo, choosing the right colors, and finding your brand's voice.

The art of storytelling for new entrepreneurs involves crafting a compelling origin story, connecting with your audience emotionally, showcasing your values, painting vivid pictures, sharing milestones and growth, engaging through various mediums, maintaining consistency and authenticity, and inviting interaction and feedback. Mastering this skill can help you authentically share your business's unique journey and create a deeper connection with your customers. The art of storytelling is a powerful tool that can help new entrepreneurs authentically share their business's unique journey. Below I go into further detail, explaining how entrepreneurs can master this skill.

1. Crafting Your Origin Story

- Start at the Beginning: Every business has a beginning. Share the story of what inspired you to start your business. What problem did you want to solve, or what opportunity did you want to seize? Explain the "why" behind your venture.

- Embrace Vulnerability: Authentic storytelling often involves being vulnerable. Share the challenges, doubts, and setbacks you encountered in the early stages. This humanizes your journey and makes it relatable to others.

2. Connecting with Your Audience

- Know Your Audience: Understand the interests, values, and pain points of your target audience. Tailor your storytelling to resonate with them. Highlight how your business addresses their needs or aspirations.

- Use Emotion: Effective stories evoke emotions. Share moments of triumph, excitement, or even moments of frustration and perseverance. Emotional connections make your story memorable.

3. Showcasing Your Values

- Highlight Your Values: Storytelling is an excellent way to convey your business's values and ethics. Share stories that demonstrate your commitment to integrity, customer satisfaction, sustainability, or any other core value.

- Walk the Talk: Ensure that your actions align with the values you promote in your stories. Authenticity is built on consistency, and customers appreciate businesses that practice what they preach.

4. Painting a Vivid Picture

- Use Descriptive Language: Paint a vivid picture with your words. Describe the sights, sounds, and emotions associated with your business journey. Make your audience feel like they're part of the story.

- Create Metaphors: Metaphorical storytelling can be powerful. Use metaphors or analogies to simplify complex concepts and make them more relatable.

5. Sharing Milestones and Growth

- Celebrate Achievements: Share stories of your business's milestones, whether it's reaching a sales target, launching a new product, or expanding into new markets. Celebrate your successes with your audience!

- Reflect on Growth: Talk about how your business has evolved over time. Share insights into the lessons you've learned and how you've adapted to changing circumstances. This showcases your ability to navigate challenges and grow.

6. Engaging Through Multiple Mediums

- Diversify Your Content: Storytelling isn't limited to written words. Use various mediums like videos, blog posts, social media updates, and even podcasts to share your stories. Different formats can reach different audiences.

- Engage with Visuals: Visual storytelling through images and videos can be highly engaging. Show behind-the-scenes glimpses of your business, introduce team members, or showcase customer testimonials.

7. Consistency and Authenticity

- Stay True to Your Brand: Your storytelling should align with your brand identity and values consistently. Authenticity is about being true to your business's essence.

- Honesty Is Key: Authenticity doesn't mean hiding flaws or challenges. If your business faced setbacks or made mistakes, acknowledge them honestly and share how you learned and improved.

8. Invite Interaction and Feedback

- Create a Dialogue: Encourage your audience to interact with your stories. Ask questions, seek feedback, and create opportunities for your customers to share their own stories and experiences.

- Listen and Adapt: Pay attention to the feedback and stories your audience shares with you. Use this input to refine your storytelling and better meet their needs.

Section 2: Creating a Memorable Logo

Choosing the right colors, and finding your brand's voice are essential steps for new entrepreneurs looking to establish a strong brand identity. Here's a guide on how to accomplish each of these:

1. Creating a Memorable Logo

- Simplicity is Key: Keep your logo design simple and easily recognizable. A cluttered or complex logo may be difficult to remember. Think of iconic logos like Apple's apple or Nike's swoosh for inspiration.

- Reflect Your Brand: Your logo should convey the essence of your business. Consider the values, mission, and personality of your brand. Do you want it to be playful, elegant, or professional? Ensure your logo aligns with these characteristics.

- Versatility: Your logo should look great in various sizes and formats, from business cards to billboards. Test your logo's scalability to ensure it remains clear and impactful.

- Uniqueness: Aim for a logo that stands out from the competition. Avoid clichés or generic design elements commonly seen in your industry.

- Color and Typography: Choose colors and fonts that complement your logo. They should enhance its overall impact. For example, if your logo features a playful design, opt for fun and friendly fonts.

2. Choosing the Right Colors

- Understand Color Psychology: Colors evoke emotions and convey messages. Research color psychology to understand how different colors are perceived. For instance, blue often represents trust and reliability, while red can symbolize energy and passion.

- Consistency is Key: Select a color palette that aligns with your brand's personality and values, and use these colors consistently across all branding materials. Consistency helps build brand recognition.

- Contrast: Ensure there's enough contrast between text and background colors in your branding materials for readability. It's essential for websites, brochures, and other content.

- Accessibility: Consider color accessibility for individuals with visual impairments. Use color contrast tools to check if your color choices are accessible to everyone.

3. Finding Your Brand's Voice

- Define Your Brand Persona: Determine the personality and tone of your brand. Is it friendly, professional, humorous, or informative? This sets the foundation for your brand's voice.

- Know Your Audience: Understand your target audience's preferences and communication style. Tailor your brand's voice to resonate with them. For example, a brand targeting young adults might adopt a more casual tone.

- Create Brand Guidelines: Establish clear brand guidelines that include voice and tone guidelines. Provide examples of how to communicate in different situations, from social media posts to customer service interactions.

- Consistency in Communication: Ensure that your brand's voice remains consistent across all channels. Whether it's your website, social media, or customer support, the way you communicate should reflect your brand's personality.

- Test and Refine: As you engage with your audience, pay attention to their reactions and feedback. Refine your brand's voice over time based on what resonates best with your audience.

Remember that creating a memorable logo, choosing the right colors, and finding your brand's voice is an ongoing process. Your brand identity may evolve as your business grows and adapts to changing market dynamics. Stay attuned to your audience and market trends to ensure that your brand remains relevant and compelling.

Section 3: Mastering Your Online Marketing

In today's digital age, online marketing is your passport to a global audience! It's not just about having an online presence; it's about making that presence count. In the following sections, we will explore strategies and techniques for online marketing. From social media mastery to content marketing excellence and the power of SEO (Search Engine Optimization), you'll gain the knowledge and skills to leave a lasting mark in the digital world.

Social media strategies that work:

I. Social Media Engagement

In social media strategies, focus on meaningful engagement rather than mere presence. Create a content calendar that fosters conversation, encourages user-generated content, and responds promptly to comments and messages.

Creating a content calendar is crucial for new entrepreneurs looking to build a strong online presence. Here's a step-by-step guide on how to create such a content calendar:

1. Define Your Content Strategy

- Know Your Audience: Understand your target audience's interests, pain points, and preferences. Tailor your content to resonate with them.

- Set Objectives: Clearly define your content marketing goals. Are you aiming to increase brand awareness, drive website traffic, or boost engagement? Knowing your objectives will guide your content choices.

- Content Themes: Identify the core themes or topics that align with your brand and appeal to your audience. These themes will serve as the foundation of your content calendar.

2. Choose Content Types

- Diversify Content: Include a variety of content types in your calendar, such as blog posts, videos, infographics, podcasts, and social media updates. Diversification keeps your audience engaged.

- User-Generated Content (UGC): Plan UGC campaigns where you encourage customers to create content related to your brand. For example, you can run a contest asking users to share photos using your product.

3. Creating a Content Calendar

- Monthly Overview: Start by creating a monthly calendar overview. This will help you visualize your content distribution and ensure a balanced mix of topics and content types.

- Editorial Calendar Tools: Use digital tools like Google Calendar, Trello, or specialized content calendar platforms like Hootsuite to organize and schedule your content. These tools can send you reminders and notifications for upcoming posts.

4. Foster Conversation

- Engagement Posts: Include posts that explicitly encourage engagement. For example, ask questions, conduct polls, or seek opinions on trending topics within your industry.

- Storytelling: Share stories and anecdotes related to your brand or industry. Stories are highly shareable and can spark conversations.

- Interactive Content: Create interactive content like quizzes, surveys, or contests to engage your audience and encourage participation.

5. Encourage User-Generated Content (UGC)

- UGC Campaigns: Plan and promote UGC campaigns. Provide clear instructions on how customers can participate and share their content. Acknowledge and feature user-generated content on your platforms.

- Use Hashtags: Create unique hashtags for your brand or campaigns. Encourage customers to use these hashtags when sharing content related to your products or services.

6. Respond Promptly

- Set Response Times: Establish a policy for responding to comments and messages on your various platforms. Aim to respond within a specific time frame, such as within 24 hours.

- Customer Support: Address customer inquiries and concerns promptly and professionally. Excellent customer service can lead to positive reviews and referrals.

7. Monitor and Analyze

- Track Metrics: Use analytics tools to monitor the performance of your content. Pay attention to metrics like engagement rates, click-through rates, and conversions.

- Feedback Loop: Continuously gather feedback from your audience. Ask for opinions and suggestions to improve your content and responsiveness.

8. Iterate and Optimize

- Learn from Data: Use the insights gained from data and audience feedback to refine your content calendar and strategy. Adjust your approach based on what works best.

- Experiment: Don't be afraid to try new content ideas and strategies. Experimentation can lead to innovative ways of fostering engagement and encouraging user-generated content.

- Remember that building an engaged online community takes time and consistent effort. By creating a well-planned content calendar that prioritizes conversation, user-generated content, and prompt responses, you can build a loyal and interactive online following for your brand.

II. Social Media Influencer Campaigns

Engaging with social media influencers can be a powerful marketing strategy for new entrepreneurs. Here's a comprehensive guide on how to effectively work with influencers to achieve great marketing results:

1. Define Your Goals: Start by clearly defining your marketing objectives. Are you looking to increase brand awareness, drive website traffic, boost sales, or promote a specific product or service? Understanding your goals will help you identify the right influencers.

2. Identify the Right Influencers: Look for influencers whose audience aligns with your target demographic and shares common interests. Consider factors such as follower count, engagement rate, content quality, and relevance to your industry.

3. Build Relationships: Establish authentic relationships with influencers by engaging with their content, commenting, and sharing their posts. Follow them on various social media platforms to show your genuine interest in their content.

4. Reach Out Thoughtfully: When reaching out to influencers, personalize your messages. Explain why you admire their work and how your collaboration can benefit both parties. Be transparent about your expectations, compensation, and deliverables.

5. Collaborate Creatively: Work closely with influencers to brainstorm creative campaign ideas that resonate with their audience. Encourage them to incorporate your product or service seamlessly into their content.

6. Set Clear Expectations: Establish clear expectations and guidelines for the collaboration. Define deliverables, posting schedules, content formats, and any key messages you want to convey.

7. Compensation and Contracts: Discuss compensation terms with influencers. Payment can vary based on factors like follower count and engagement rates. Ensure you have a written contract that outlines all terms and conditions.

8. Content Review and Approval: Request to review the content before it's published. This allows you to ensure that your brand message is conveyed accurately and that it aligns with your goals.

9. Disclosure and Transparency: Ensure that influencers clearly disclose their partnerships with your brand as per legal and industry guidelines. Transparency builds trust with their audience.

10. Monitor and Measure: Track the performance of your influencer campaigns using key performance indicators (KPIs) relevant to your goals. Metrics can include engagement rates, website traffic, sales conversions, and ROI.

11. Engage with the Audience: Encourage the influencer to engage with their audience through comments, responses to questions, and interaction with your brand. This creates a sense of authenticity and trust.

12. Long-Term Relationships: Consider building long-term relationships with influencers who consistently deliver results. Repeat collaborations can strengthen brand loyalty and recognition.

13. Adapt and Learn: Continuously assess the performance of your influencer marketing efforts and be willing to adapt your strategy based on what works best for your brand.

14. Legal and Compliance: Familiarize yourself with the legal and ethical guidelines for influencer marketing in your region. Ensure that your campaigns comply with all relevant regulations.

15. Diversify Your Influencer Pool: Don't rely solely on one influencer. Diversify your influencer pool to reach a broader audience and mitigate risks associated with changes in algorithms or influencer availability.

Remember that successful influencer marketing is built on trust, authenticity, and mutual benefit. By approaching influencer collaborations strategically and ethically, you can harness the power of social media influencers to achieve excellent marketing results for your business.

III. Social Listening and Insights

Harness the power of social listening tools to monitor conversations and trends related to your industry and brand. Use insights to refine your content strategy and stay ahead of the curve.

Harnessing the power of social listening tools is a valuable practice for new entrepreneurs. It allows you to monitor conversations and trends related to your industry and brand, gaining valuable insights, and refining your content strategy to stay ahead of the curve. Here's a step-by-step guide on how to do this effectively:

1. Choose the Right Social Listening Tools

- **Research Tools:** Explore social listening tools like Brandwatch, Hootsuite, Mention, or Google Alerts. Select a tool that aligns with your budget and specific monitoring needs.

2. Set Up Relevant Keywords and Alerts

- **Identify Keywords:** Determine the keywords, phrases, hashtags, and mentions relevant to your industry, brand, products, and competitors. These will be the triggers for your social listening alerts.

- **Create Alerts:** Set up alerts within your chosen social listening tool to monitor these keywords across various social media platforms, blogs, forums, news sites, and other online channels.

3. Monitor Conversations and Trends

- **Real-Time Monitoring:** Regularly check your social listening tool for real-time updates on mentions, conversations, and trending topics related to your industry.

- **Competitor Analysis:** Use the tool to monitor what your competitors are doing and how their audience is responding. Analyze their content strategies and identify gaps or opportunities.

- Track Industry Trends: Stay informed about industry trends, emerging topics, and shifts in consumer sentiment. Identify influential voices and thought leaders in your field.

4. Analyze and Extract Insights

- Categorize Mentions: Group mentions and conversations into categories such as positive, negative, or neutral sentiment. This helps you gauge overall sentiment around your brand and industry.

- Identify Pain Points: Pay attention to customer complaints, feedback, and pain points. These insights can guide product improvements or content creation to address customer needs.

- Spot Emerging Trends: Look for recurring themes or emerging trends in conversations. Identify topics that are gaining traction and may become important in your industry.

5. Refine Your Content Strategy

- Content Optimization: Use the insights gained from social listening to optimize your content strategy. Tailor your content to address the pain points, questions, and interests of your audience.

- Content Personalization: Create personalized content that resonates with specific segments of your audience based on their preferences and needs.

- Trend Integration: Incorporate trending topics and relevant industry trends into your content to demonstrate your brand's relevance and awareness.

6. Engage in Conversations

- Join Discussions: Participate in relevant conversations by responding to comments and engaging with your audience. Address questions and provide value through meaningful interactions.

- Show Empathy: Show empathy when responding to customer feedback, whether it's positive or negative. Acknowledging and addressing concerns can build trust.

7. Stay Ahead of the Curve

- Continuous Monitoring: Social listening is an ongoing practice. Keep monitoring conversations and trends to stay updated on industry developments and shifts in customer sentiment.

- Adapt and Innovate: Use the insights you gather to adapt your strategies and innovate. Being agile in response to changing trends can help you stay ahead of the competition.

By harnessing the power of social listening tools and using the insights obtained to refine your content strategy, you can build a more effective and customer-centric approach to marketing and brand management. This not only keeps you informed about industry trends but also allows you to proactively respond to your audience's needs and preferences.

IV. Micro-Moments Marketing

Embrace micro-moments marketing, where you deliver content and solutions to users at the exact moment they need it. This requires a deep understanding of user intent and timely, personalized responses.

Micro-moments marketing is a powerful strategy for new entrepreneurs looking to engage with their audience by delivering content and solutions at the exact moment users need them. It revolves around understanding user intent and providing timely, personalized responses. Here's a step-by-step guide on how to implement micro-moments marketing effectively:

1. Understand User Intent

- Identify Micro-Moments: Recognize the various micro-moments that users experience throughout their customer journey. These can include "I-want-to-know" moments (researching), "I-want-to-go" moments (locating a business), "I-want-to-do" moments (learning how to do something), and "I-want-to-buy" moments (making a purchase decision).

- User Persona Analysis: Develop detailed user personas to understand your audience's needs, pain points, and behaviors during these micro-moments. Conduct surveys, interviews, and market research to gather insights.

- Keyword Research: Use keyword research tools to identify the specific search queries and phrases users are entering during these micro-moments. This helps you align your content with their intent.

2. Create Relevant Content

- Tailor Content: Develop content that directly addresses the questions or needs associated with each micro-moment. Content can include blog posts, videos, infographics, FAQs, tutorials, and more.

- Mobile Optimization: Ensure that your content is mobile-friendly and loads quickly, as many micro-moments happen on mobile devices.

- Local SEO: If applicable to your business, optimize for local search to capture "near me" micro-moments. This includes maintaining accurate business listings, acquiring online reviews, and creating location-specific content.

3. Implement Timely Responses

- Real-Time Engagement: Monitor your online channels (website, social media, email) in real-time to identify and respond promptly to user inquiries and comments.

- Chatbots and Automation: Consider implementing chatbots and automation tools to provide instant responses during micro-moments when human interaction isn't required.

4. Personalize Responses

- **User Data Utilization:** Leverage user data and behavior tracking to personalize responses and recommendations. For example, if a user frequently searches for fitness content, offer workout plans or nutrition tips during relevant micro-moments.

- **Email Marketing:** Use email marketing to send personalized recommendations or offers based on user interactions and preferences.

5. Measure and Optimize

- **Analytics Tracking:** Implement analytics tools to track user interactions and conversions during micro-moments. Identify which content and responses are most effective.

V. Implementing Analytics Tools

Implementing analytics tools to track user interactions and conversions during micro-moments is essential for new entrepreneurs. It helps you gain insights into the effectiveness of your micro-moments marketing strategy and enables data-driven decision-making. Here's a step-by-step guide on how to do this effectively:

1. Choose the Right Analytics Tools

- **Select a Platform:** Start by choosing an analytics platform that suits your business needs and budget. Google Analytics is a popular choice for web-based analytics, while social media platforms offer built-in analytics for their channels.

- Consider Specialized Tools: Depending on your business and marketing channels, you may benefit from specialized analytics tools that provide more detailed insights into specific areas, such as social media analytics tools or email marketing analytics platforms.

2. Set Up Analytics Tracking

- Website Integration: If you have a website, integrate your chosen analytics tool by adding tracking codes (e.g., Google Analytics tracking code) to your website's pages. Follow the tool's specific instructions for implementation.

- Tagging and Tracking: Use UTM parameters or tagging to track specific micro-moment campaigns or content. This allows you to attribute user interactions and conversions to specific micro-moments.

VI. UTM parameters

UTM parameters, or Urchin Tracking Module parameters, are tags that you can add to your website URLs to track specific information about the source, medium, campaign, and other attributes of traffic to your site. They are particularly useful for measuring the effectiveness of marketing campaigns, including micro-moment campaigns. Here's an explanation of UTM parameters and how to use tagging to track micro-moment campaigns or content:

1. UTM Parameters Explained

UTM parameters are extra information added to the end of a URL. When someone clicks on a URL with UTM parameters, the information is sent to your analytics tools, allowing you to track and analyze the source of the traffic.

2. Components of UTM Parameters

UTM parameters consist of several key components:

- Source: This indicates where the traffic is coming from, such as a specific social media platform (e.g., Facebook, Twitter) or a particular website.

- Medium: This represents the type of traffic source, such as social, email, or referral.

- Campaign: This identifies the specific marketing campaign or initiative that the URL is associated with.

- Term (optional): Used for paid search campaigns to track keywords.

- Content (optional): Used to differentiate between different pieces of content within the same campaign.

3. Benefits of Using UTM Parameters

By using UTM parameters, you can:

- Identify which marketing channels are driving the most traffic to your website.

- Measure the success of specific campaigns or content pieces.

- Understand user behavior and conversion rates for each traffic source.

- Fine-tune your marketing strategies based on data-driven insights.

4. Using Tagging for Micro-Moment Campaigns

When running micro-moment campaigns (short, real-time interactions with your audience), tagging becomes crucial for tracking their performance. Here's how to do it:

- Create a unique UTM parameter for each micro-moment campaign. For example, if you're running a real-time flash sale on Instagram, you can create a UTM parameter with "source=instagram," "medium=social," and "campaign=flash-sale."

- Generate tagged URLs using tools like Google's Campaign URL Builder or URL shorteners like Bitly. These tools help you create URLs with UTM parameters added.

- Share these tagged URLs in your micro-moment content. When users click on the links, the UTM parameters will track their interactions.

5. Analyzing the Results

After running your micro-moment campaigns with tagged URLs, you can analyze the data in your analytics platform (e.g., Google Analytics). Look for insights such as which micro-moment campaigns generated the most clicks, conversions, or engagement.

6. Optimization and Iteration

Use the data gathered through UTM parameters to optimize your micro-moment campaigns. If one type of micro-moment content performs exceptionally well, you can allocate more resources to similar campaigns in the future.

In summary, UTM parameters are a valuable tool for tracking the effectiveness of micro-moment campaigns and other marketing initiatives. By strategically tagging your URLs with UTM parameters, you can gain valuable insights into the performance of your micro-moment content and make data-driven decisions to improve your marketing efforts.

VII. Continually Improve Your Campaigns

1. Define Key Metrics:

- Identify Goals: Determine what specific actions or outcomes you want to track during micro-moments. These could include website visits, form submissions, email sign-ups, purchases, or other relevant conversions.

- Micro-Moment Metrics: Define micro-moment-specific metrics, such as click-through rates (CTR), conversion rates, bounce rates, and engagement metrics (likes, shares, comments, etc.).

2. Track User Interactions

- Website Behavior: Use analytics to monitor user behavior on your website during micro-moments. Track the pages they visit, the duration of their visits, and the actions they take (e.g., clicking on links, watching videos).

- Event Tracking: Implement event tracking for specific micro-moment actions, such as clicking a "Learn More" button or watching a tutorial video. This helps you understand how users interact with your content.

3. Monitor Conversions

- Conversion Tracking: Set up conversion tracking to measure how many users complete desired actions during micro-moments. For instance, if you want users to sign up for your newsletter, track the number of sign-ups generated during a specific micro-moment campaign.

- E-commerce Tracking: If you're an e-commerce business, enable e-commerce tracking to monitor sales and revenue generated as a result of micro-moments.

4. Generate Reports and Insights

- **Regular Reporting:** Schedule regular reporting intervals (e.g., weekly, monthly) to review the performance of your micro-moments marketing campaigns and content.

- **Custom Reports:** Create custom reports or dashboards within your analytics tool to focus on micro-moment-specific metrics and conversions.

5. Analyze and Optimize

- **Data Analysis:** Analyze the data collected through your analytics tools to gain insights into what's working and what needs improvement during micro-moments.

- **Identify Trends:** Look for trends in user behavior and conversion rates across different micro-moments. Identify which micro-moments are most effective in driving desired actions.

- **A/B Testing:** Conduct A/B testing to experiment with different content or strategies during micro-moments. Measure the impact of changes on user interactions and conversions.

6. A/B Testing

- A/B testing, also known as split testing, is a method used in marketing and web development to compare two different versions of a webpage, email, or other content to determine which one performs better in achieving a specific goal.

Here's how it works:

- Creation of Variations: Two versions of the content are created: the original (A) and a modified version (B). These versions differ in one or more elements, such as headlines, images, call-to-action buttons, or overall design.

- Randomized Distribution: Users are randomly divided into two groups. Group A is exposed to version A, while Group B is exposed to version B.

- Performance Measurement: Metrics related to the content's goal are tracked and measured for both versions. Common goals include click-through rates, conversion rates, engagement, or sales.

- Comparison: After a sufficient number of users have interacted with both versions, the performance of each is compared. The version that performs better in achieving the goal is typically chosen as the winner.

- Implementation: The winning version (A or B) is implemented as the standard content, and future users are exposed to it.

A/B testing allows businesses to make data-driven decisions by understanding how specific changes impact user behavior and outcomes. It's a valuable tool for optimizing websites, emails, ads, and other marketing materials to improve conversion rates and overall effectiveness.

7. Adapt Your Strategy

- Data-Driven Decisions: Use the insights from analytics to make data-driven decisions. Adjust your micro-moments marketing strategy based on what the data tells you.

- Continuous Optimization: Micro-moments marketing is an ongoing process. Continuously optimize your approach based on the performance data you gather over time.

By effectively implementing analytics tools and tracking user interactions and conversions during micro-moments, new entrepreneurs can refine their strategies, allocate resources efficiently, and ultimately drive better results from their micro-moment marketing efforts.

VIII. Be Helpful, Not Salesy

- Provide Value: Focus on delivering value and solutions to users during micro-moments rather than pushing sales. Building trust and establishing your brand as a helpful resource will lead to long-term customer loyalty.

IX. Adapt to Changing Trends

- Stay Current: Stay updated on industry trends, user behavior changes, and emerging micro-moments. Be prepared to adapt your strategy accordingly.

X. Consistency Across Channels

- Ensure Consistency: Maintain a consistent brand voice and messaging across all online channels to reinforce your brand identity during micro-moments.

Embracing micro-moments marketing requires a deep understanding of your audience's needs and behaviors. By delivering relevant, timely, and personalized content and responses, you can meet users at the right moment, build stronger connections, and drive engagement and conversions.

Section 4: Content Marketing Excellence

I. Content Creation

Elevate your content marketing by delving into content formats. Experiment with interactive content such as quizzes, calculators, and 360-degree videos to engage your audience more deeply.

1. Quizzes

- Audience Engagement: Quizzes are highly engaging because they invite audience participation. Entrepreneurs can create quizzes related to their industry, products, or services that challenge users' knowledge or help them discover something about themselves.

- Lead Generation: Quizzes can be used strategically for lead generation. Require users to enter their email addresses to see their quiz results, thereby building your email list.

- Content Personalization: Quizzes allow you to deliver personalized results and recommendations based on users' quiz answers. This personalized approach can enhance the user experience and drive conversions.

- Promotion: Promote your quizzes on your website, social media channels, and email newsletters to maximize reach. Encourage users to share their quiz results on social media, which can increase visibility and engagement.

2. Calculators

- Practical Utility: Calculators provide practical value to users. Entrepreneurs can create calculators that help users make informed decisions related to their products or services. For example, a financial advisor could offer a mortgage calculator.

- Data Collection: Like quizzes, calculators can be used for lead generation. Ask users to input their information (e.g., financial details) to get personalized results, and collect their contact information for follow-up.

- Visual Appeal: Make your calculators visually appealing and user-friendly. Use intuitive design and clear instructions to ensure users can easily navigate and input data.

- SEO Benefits: Well-optimized calculator pages can also attract organic traffic through search engines. Ensure that you use relevant keywords and meta tags for SEO purposes.

3. 360-Degree Videos

- Immersive Experience: 360-degree videos provide an immersive experience that can captivate your audience. Use them to showcase your products, services, or behind-the-scenes glimpses of your business.

- Virtual Tours: If you have a physical location or offer experiences that can be showcased visually, consider creating virtual tours using 360-degree videos. This is particularly useful for businesses in the travel, real estate, or hospitality sectors.

- Social Media: Share 360-degree videos on social media platforms that support this format, such as Facebook and YouTube. These videos tend to receive higher engagement and shares.

- Storytelling: Use 360-degree videos to tell compelling stories. They allow viewers to explore the environment and interact with elements in the video, creating a unique storytelling opportunity.

4. Measuring and Iterating

- Analytics: Track the performance of your interactive content using analytics tools. Monitor user engagement, conversion rates, and other relevant metrics to assess the impact of your content.

- User Feedback: Encourage users to provide feedback on the interactive content. This can offer valuable insights for improvement.

- Iterate: Based on data and user feedback, iterate on your interactive content. Make improvements to enhance user experience and achieve your business objectives.

- Interactive content formats like quizzes, calculators, and 360-degree videos can set your business apart and foster deeper engagement with your audience. When used strategically and creatively, they can be valuable tools for achieving your marketing and business goals.

II. Storytelling Through Content

Use storytelling techniques to create compelling narratives around your brand and products. Storytelling weaves a cohesive brand story throughout your content strategy.

1. Know Your Audience

Before crafting your narrative, understand your target audience. What are their interests, pain points, and aspirations? Tailor your story to resonate with their needs and values.

2. Define Your Brand's Core Values

Identify the core values that drive your brand. What does your brand stand for, and what principles guide your business? Your story should align with these values.

3. Craft a Unique Origin Story

Share the story of how your business came to be. Highlight the problem or inspiration that led to its creation. People love to hear about the passion and purpose behind a brand.

4. Create a Hero's Journey

Position your brand or product as the hero on a journey. Every good story has a protagonist facing challenges and striving for a goal. Highlight how your brand helps customers overcome obstacles and achieve their desires.

5. Use Emotion

Emotions are a key element of effective storytelling. Appeal to your audience's emotions by creating relatable characters, situations, and outcomes. Whether it's joy, empathy, or inspiration, evoke feelings that resonate with your brand's message.

6. Be Authentic

Authenticity is vital in storytelling. Don't embellish or exaggerate. Share real experiences, successes, and even failures. Authenticity builds trust with your audience.

7. Showcase Customer Stories

Share success stories of customers who have benefited from your product or service. Use testimonials and case studies to demonstrate how your brand has made a positive impact in real people's lives.

8. Create a Narrative Arc

Structure your storytelling with a beginning, middle, and end. Start with a setup that introduces the situation, present the conflict or challenge, and conclude with a resolution or transformation.

9. Use Visuals

Incorporate visual elements into your storytelling, such as images, videos, and infographics. Visuals can enhance the emotional impact of your narrative.

10. Consistency Across Channels

Maintain consistency in your storytelling across all marketing channels, including your website, social media, email campaigns, and offline materials. A unified narrative strengthens your brand identity.

11. Foster Engagement

Encourage audience engagement by asking questions, inviting comments, and encouraging user-generated content. Engagement can extend the reach of your brand's story.

12. Adapt to Different Formats

Tailor your narrative to various content formats, such as blog posts, videos, podcasts, and social media updates. Different formats allow you to reach a broader audience.

13. Measure Impact

Use analytics tools to measure the impact of your storytelling efforts. Monitor metrics like engagement rates, website traffic, and conversion rates to gauge the effectiveness of your narratives.

14. Iterate and Evolve

Storytelling is an ongoing process. Continually refine and evolve your narratives based on feedback and changing audience preferences.

Effective storytelling can not only capture your audience's attention but also foster a deeper connection between your brand and your customers. By weaving compelling narratives around your brand and products, you can create a memorable and meaningful presence in the market.

III. User-Generated Content Campaigns

Encourage your customers to become content creators themselves. Run user-generated content campaigns that showcase real experiences with your products or services. Here's a step-by-step guide on how to run such campaigns effectively:

1. Define Your UGC Campaign Goals

Start by clearly defining the goals of your UGC campaign. Are you looking to increase brand awareness, boost engagement, drive sales, or gather customer testimonials? Knowing your objectives will help shape your campaign strategy.

2. Identify Your Target Audience

Determine the specific audience you want to engage with your UGC campaign. Understanding your audience's demographics, interests, and preferences will guide your content and outreach efforts.

3. Create Clear Campaign Guidelines

Develop clear and concise guidelines for participants. These guidelines should include instructions on what type of content you're looking for, any relevant hashtags or keywords to use, and how to submit their content.

4. Choose the Right UGC Platform

Select the most suitable platform(s) for your UGC campaign. Social media platforms like Instagram, Twitter, and TikTok are popular choices, but consider other options like your website, email newsletters, or even dedicated UGC platforms.

5. Leverage Hashtags and Tags

Create a unique and branded hashtag for your campaign. Encourage participants to use this hashtag when sharing their content. Additionally, tag participants in your posts to give credit and show appreciation for their contributions.

6. Offer Incentives

To motivate users to participate, consider offering incentives such as discounts, exclusive access, or the chance to be featured prominently on your platform. Make the rewards appealing and relevant to your audience.

7. Encourage Storytelling

Encourage participants to share their personal stories and experiences related to your products or services. Authentic and heartfelt stories can resonate deeply with your audience.

8. Curate and Showcase UGC

Regularly curate and showcase the best UGC on your website, social media profiles, or other marketing channels. Highlighting user-generated content demonstrates social proof and builds trust.

9. Engage and Respond

Actively engage with participants by responding to their content, thanking them, and asking questions. Show genuine interest in their experiences and feedback.

10. Monitor and Moderate

Continuously monitor UGC submissions to ensure they align with your brand guidelines and campaign objectives. Be prepared to moderate and remove inappropriate or off-topic content.

11. Promote Sharing and Interaction

Encourage users to share and interact with each other's UGC. Host contests or challenges that involve sharing UGC and tagging friends, further expanding your campaign's reach.

12. Measure and Analyze

Use analytics tools to measure the impact of your UGC campaign. Track metrics such as engagement rates, website traffic, conversions, and user-generated content volume. Analyze the data to assess the campaign's success and areas for improvement.

13. Legal Considerations

Ensure that you have the necessary rights to use user-generated content in your marketing materials. Seek permission from participants to feature their content, and clearly communicate how it will be used.

14. Express Gratitude

Don't forget to express gratitude to your customers for their contributions. Publicly acknowledge and thank them for being a part of your brand's journey.

Running UGC campaigns can not only create authentic connections with your audience but also serve as valuable social proof for potential customers. When executed effectively, these campaigns can enhance your brand's credibility and engagement levels.

Section 5: The Power of SEO (Search Engine Optimization)

I. Keyword Research

In SEO, conduct extensive keyword research using tools and techniques. Focus on long-tail keywords, question-based queries, and semantic search to capture niche audiences.

Here's a step-by-step guide on how to do this:

1. Understand the Basics

- Learn SEO Fundamentals: Familiarize yourself with the basics of SEO (Search Engine Optimization), including on-page optimization, off-page optimization, and technical SEO.

2. Keyword Research

- Use Tools: Invest in keyword research tools such as Ahrefs, SEMrush, Moz, or Ubersuggest. These tools provide in-depth insights into keyword competition, search volume, and trends.

- Focus on Long-Tail Keywords: Long-tail keywords are longer and more specific search phrases that typically have lower competition and higher conversion potential. Identify relevant long-tail keywords related to your niche.

- Question-Based Queries: Consider question-based queries that users might search for within your niche. Tools like

AnswerThePublic can help you find common questions related to your industry.

- Semantic Search: Understand semantic search, which is how search engines interpret the context and intent behind user queries. Use tools like LSIGraph to identify semantically related keywords to your main target keywords.

3. Competitor Analysis

- Analyze Competitors: Study your competitors' websites and content to identify keywords they are ranking for. Tools like SEMrush allow you to track competitors' keyword rankings.

- Identify Content Gaps: Look for keyword opportunities that your competitors might have missed. Create content targeting these keywords to capture niche audiences.

4. Content Creation

- Quality Content: Develop high-quality, informative, and engaging content that caters to the keywords and topics you've identified. Ensure that your content adds value to your niche audience.

- Optimize for Long-Tail Keywords: Incorporate long-tail keywords naturally into your content, including in headings, subheadings, and the body of your articles. Avoid keyword stuffing.

- Answer Questions: Address common questions and concerns related to your niche within your content. Use question-based queries as inspiration for creating informative articles and guides.

5. On-Page SEO

- Meta Tags: Optimize your meta titles and descriptions to include relevant long-tail keywords and phrases. Ensure that they accurately represent the content.

- Header Tags: Use header tags (H1, H2, H3) to structure your content logically. Include keywords in headings when relevant.

- Image Optimization: Optimize images with descriptive alt text and filenames that contain keywords.

6. Technical SEO

- Site Speed: Ensure your website loads quickly to provide a better user experience. Use tools like Google PageSpeed Insights to identify and fix speed issues.

- Mobile Optimization: Make sure your website is mobile-friendly as mobile users are a significant portion of internet traffic.

- Schema Markup: Implement schema markup to provide search engines with structured data that enhances search results.

7. Track and Adjust

- Monitor Performance: Use Google Analytics and search engine ranking tools to monitor keyword performance and website traffic.

- Adjust Your Strategy: Based on your analysis, adjust your content, keywords, and SEO strategy to optimize your rankings and capture niche audiences more effectively.

Remember that SEO is an ongoing process, and results may take time to materialize. Consistency, patience, and a commitment to providing value to your niche audience are key to success in SEO.

II. Technical SEO Mastery

Dive into technical SEO, addressing issues such as website speed, mobile optimization, schema markup, and structured data. A technically optimized website enhances user experience and search engine visibility.

Diving into technical SEO is crucial for new entrepreneurs looking to improve their website's performance and search engine rankings. Technical SEO focuses on the behind-the-scenes aspects of your website that impact its visibility on search engines. Here's a step-by-step guide on how to address key technical SEO issues:

1. Website Speed Optimization

- Use Page Speed Tools: Start by using tools like Google PageSpeed Insights or GTmetrix to assess your website's current speed performance. These tools provide recommendations for improvement.

- Compress Images: Large images can slow down your website. Compress images before uploading them to your site, or use image compression plugins if you're using a content management system (CMS) like WordPress.

- Leverage Browser Caching: Enable browser caching to store frequently used resources on a user's device, reducing the need to re-download them on subsequent visits.

- Minimize HTTP Requests: Reduce the number of HTTP requests by combining and minimizing CSS and JavaScript files. Use asynchronous loading for non-essential scripts.

- Choose a Fast Hosting Provider: Select a reliable hosting provider that offers fast server response times. Consider using a Content Delivery Network (CDN) to distribute content across multiple servers.

2. Mobile Optimization

- Mobile-First Design: Ensure that your website is designed with a mobile-first approach. It should be responsive and adapt seamlessly to various screen sizes and devices.

- Mobile-Friendly Testing: Use Google's Mobile-Friendly Test to check if your site meets mobile usability standards. Address any issues identified in the test results.

- Accelerated Mobile Pages (AMP): Consider implementing AMP for content-heavy pages like blog posts and articles to improve mobile load times.

3. Schema Markup and Structured Data

- Learn About Schema Markup: Familiarize yourself with schema markup, which is a structured data vocabulary used by search engines to understand the content of web pages.

- Identify Relevant Markup: Determine which types of schema markup are relevant to your content and business. Common types include product, recipe, event, and organization markup.

- Implement Markup: Add schema markup to your website's HTML code. You can do this manually or use plugins or tools that generate the markup for you.

- Validate Markup: Use Google's Structured Data Testing Tool to validate your markup and ensure it's error-free.

4. Improve Website Security

- SSL Certificate: Install an SSL certificate to secure your website and enable HTTPS. Google favors secure websites in search rankings.

- Regular Updates: Keep your website's CMS, plugins, and themes up to date to patch security vulnerabilities.

- Security Plugins: Consider using security plugins or services to enhance protection against malware and hacking attempts.

5. XML Sitemaps

- Generate XML Sitemaps: Create XML sitemaps for your website to help search engines index your pages more efficiently. Most CMS platforms offer plugins to generate sitemaps automatically.

- Submit to Search Engines: Submit your XML sitemap to search engines like Google and Bing through their webmaster tools or search console interfaces.

6. Monitor and Test

- Google Search Console: Set up Google Search Console for your website to monitor technical issues, track indexing, and receive alerts about potential problems.

- Regular Testing: Continuously test your website's performance and user experience. Use tools like Google's Mobile-Friendly Test, PageSpeed Insights, and Structured Data Testing Tool.

By addressing technical SEO issues such as website speed, mobile optimization, schema markup, and structured data, you can improve your website's search engine visibility, user experience, and overall performance. Regular monitoring and maintenance are essential to ensure your website remains optimized for both users and search engines.

III. Content SEO and Link Building

Develop content SEO strategies that include optimizing content for featured snippets and rich snippets. Explore link-building techniques, including outreach to high-authority websites.

Developing content SEO strategies and exploring link-building techniques are essential for new entrepreneurs aiming to boost their website's visibility and authority in search engine results. Here's a step-by-step guide:

Content SEO Strategies

1. Optimize for Featured Snippets

- Understand Featured Snippets: Featured snippets are concise answers to user queries that appear at the top of search results. Research the types of featured snippets common in your niche.

- Identify Snippet Opportunities: Review the existing content on your website and identify opportunities to create content that answers specific questions concisely. Use tools like SEMrush or Moz to find potential snippet opportunities.

- Structure Content: Structure your content with clear headings, bullet points, and numbered lists to make it snippet-friendly. Use schema markup where appropriate to provide structured data that search engines can understand.

- Provide Direct Answers: Craft content that directly answers common questions in your niche. Use the "People Also Ask" section in search results for inspiration.

2. Optimize for Rich Snippets

- Understand Rich Snippets: Rich snippets provide additional information in search results, such as star ratings for reviews, cooking times for recipes, or event details. Identify the types of rich snippets relevant to your content.

- Structured Data Markup: Implement structured data markup (schema.org) to help search engines understand and display your content as rich snippets. Use tools like Google's Structured Data Markup Helper to generate the markup.

- Test and Validate: Use Google's Rich Results Test to validate your structured data and see how your content will appear as a rich snippet in search results.

Link-Building Techniques

1. Identify High-Authority Websites

- Research Relevant Websites: Identify high-authority websites in your niche or related industries. These should be reputable, established websites with a strong online presence.

- Use SEO Tools: Utilize SEO tools like Ahrefs, Moz, or SEMrush to find websites with high domain authority (DA) and a good backlink profile. Look for websites that link to content similar to yours.

2. Outreach to High-Authority Websites

- Create Exceptional Content: Develop high-quality, informative, and valuable content on your website that offers something unique or enhances existing discussions in your niche.

- Craft Outreach Messages: Reach out to the owners or editors of high-authority websites with personalized and compelling outreach messages. Highlight how your content can benefit their audience.

- Guest Posting: Offer to write guest posts for these websites with a link back to your relevant, valuable content. Ensure that your guest posts align with the host website's content and guidelines.

- Collaborate and Network: Build relationships within your industry by attending conferences, webinars, and networking events. Collaborate with influencers and other entrepreneurs to increase your visibility.

3. Monitor and Measure

- Track Backlinks: Use backlink monitoring tools to keep track of new backlinks to your website. Monitor the anchor text and source of these links.

- Monitor Rankings: Continuously monitor your website's search engine rankings for relevant keywords. Tools like Google Analytics and Google Search Console can provide valuable insights.

- Analyze Traffic and Conversions: Measure the impact of your SEO and link-building efforts on website traffic, user engagement, and conversions. Adjust your strategies based on performance data.

Content SEO strategies and link-building techniques require time, effort, and a commitment to providing value to your audience and collaborating with authoritative sources. Consistency and data-driven decision-making are key to success in these endeavors.

Section 6: Analytics and Measurement

I. Data-Driven Decision-Making

Embrace a data-driven approach to online marketing. Analytics tools provide deep insights into user behavior, allowing you to refine your strategies based on concrete data.

Embracing a data-driven approach to online marketing is essential for new entrepreneurs looking to make informed decisions and optimize their marketing strategies. Here's a step-by-step guide on how to do this:

1. Set Clear Objectives

- Define Your Goals: Start by clearly defining your marketing objectives. What are you trying to achieve? Whether it's increasing website traffic, boosting conversions, or improving user engagement, your goals should be specific, measurable, achievable, relevant, and time-bound (SMART).

2. Choose the Right Analytics Tools

- Google Analytics: Implement Google Analytics on your website. It's a powerful, free tool that provides in-depth insights into user behavior, traffic sources, and more.

- Marketing Automation Platforms: If you're using marketing automation tools like HubSpot, Marketo, or Mailchimp, leverage their analytics features to track campaign performance.

- Social Media Insights: Each social media platform offers its own analytics dashboard. Use them to monitor the performance of your social media campaigns.

- Additional Tools: Consider other analytics tools like Mixpanel, Kissmetrics, or Hotjar, depending on your needs and budget.

3. Set Up Tracking and Measurement

- Conversion Tracking: Implement conversion tracking on your website to monitor specific actions users take, such as form submissions, purchases, or sign-ups.

- Event Tracking: Use event tracking to monitor user interactions like clicks on specific buttons, video views, or downloads.

- E-commerce Tracking: If you have an e-commerce website, set up e-commerce tracking to measure sales, revenue, and product performance.

4. Analyze User Behavior

- Audience Segmentation: Segment your website visitors into different groups based on demographics, location, behavior, and other relevant factors.

- User Flow Analysis: Use tools like Google Analytics to analyze the paths users take on your website. Identify drop-off points and areas where users engage the most.

- Heatmaps: Utilize heatmap tools like Hotjar to visualize where users are clicking, moving their cursors, and spending the most time on your website.

5. Refine Your Strategies Based on Data

- Data Review: Regularly review the data collected from your analytics tools. Look for patterns, trends, and insights that can guide your marketing decisions.

- A/B Testing: Conduct A/B tests to compare different marketing strategies, content variations, or website elements. Use the data to determine which performs better and make adjustments accordingly.

- Iterative Approach: Embrace an iterative approach to marketing. Continuously refine your strategies based on the data you collect. Test new ideas and tactics and measure their impact.

6. Monitor Key Performance Indicators (KPIs)

- Identify Key Metrics: Determine the key performance indicators (KPIs) that align with your marketing goals. These could include website traffic, click-through rates (CTR), conversion rates, bounce rates, and more.

- Dashboard Creation: Create customized dashboards within your analytics tools to track and visualize your KPIs. This makes it easier to monitor progress.

7. Data-Driven Decision-Making

- Regular Reporting: Develop a reporting schedule to share insights and data with your team or stakeholders regularly. This ensures everyone is informed and aligned.

- Data-Backed Strategies: Base your marketing strategies and campaigns on concrete data and insights rather than assumptions or gut feelings.

- Continuous Learning: Stay updated on the latest industry trends and advancements in analytics. Attend webinars, read industry blogs, and take courses to enhance your analytics skills.

By embracing a data-driven approach to online marketing, you'll be better equipped to understand user behavior, optimize your strategies, and ultimately achieve your marketing objectives more effectively. Data-driven decision-making is a powerful tool for entrepreneurial success in the digital landscape.

II. Attribution Modeling

Implement attribution models to understand the full customer journey. This helps you allocate resources effectively across various marketing channels.

Implementing attribution models is crucial for new entrepreneurs to gain a deeper understanding of the customer journey and allocate marketing resources effectively. Attribution models help you determine which marketing channels and touchpoints contribute the most to conversions. Here's a step-by-step guide on how to do this:

1. Understand Attribution Models

- Learn the Basics: Familiarize yourself with different attribution models, including first-touch, last-touch, linear, time decay, and algorithmic models (e.g., Markov chain or data-driven attribution).

- Understanding various attribution models is essential for new entrepreneurs looking to evaluate the effectiveness of their marketing channels and optimize their strategies. Here's an explanation of the common attribution models:

  i. First-Touch Attribution Model: In the first-touch model, all credit for a conversion or sale is attributed to the first interaction a customer had with your brand. This model helps you identify the initial touchpoints that introduce customers to your business.

  ii. Last-Touch Attribution Model: The last-touch model assigns all credit to the final interaction before a conversion or sale. It focuses on the touchpoints immediately preceding the desired action and is useful for identifying what directly led to the conversion.

  iii. Linear Attribution Model: In the linear model, credit is evenly distributed across all touchpoints a customer interacts with throughout their journey. This approach provides a more balanced view of how different channels contribute to conversions.

iv. Time Decay Attribution Model: The time decay model gives more credit to touchpoints that occurred closer in time to the conversion event. It assumes that interactions that happened just before the conversion had a more significant impact.

v. Algorithmic Attribution Models: Algorithmic attribution models use algorithms, such as Markov chains or data-driven attribution, to analyze the entire customer journey and assign credit based on statistical models. These models consider multiple touchpoints, their sequence, and their individual impact on conversions.

vi. Markov Chain Attribution: Markov chain attribution uses a probabilistic model to assess the probability of each touchpoint leading to a conversion. It considers the entire customer journey and assigns credit accordingly.

vii. Data-Driven Attribution: Data-driven attribution relies on machine learning and data analysis to determine the contribution of each touchpoint. It considers a wide range of variables and data points to create a customized attribution model for your business.

To familiarize yourself with these attribution models:

- Review Historical Data: Examine past customer journeys and conversion data to see how different attribution models would assign credit.

- Use Attribution Software: Invest in attribution software or tools that can help you implement and analyze these models. Google Analytics and marketing automation platforms often offer attribution reporting.

- Test Different Models: Experiment with different attribution models to gain insights into how each impacts your understanding of customer behavior and channel effectiveness.

- Consider Your Business Goals: Choose the attribution model that aligns best with your business objectives. For example, if brand awareness is crucial, first-touch or linear models may be more suitable.

- Regularly Evaluate and Adjust: Attribution modeling is not static. Regularly evaluate and adjust your approach based on changing customer behavior and marketing strategies.

- Understanding attribution models allows you to allocate your marketing budget more effectively, optimize your campaigns, and make data-driven decisions to drive business growth.

- Customer Journey: Understand that customer journeys are rarely linear. Customers interact with various marketing touchpoints before converting.

2. Define Your Goals

- Specific Objectives: Clearly define your business objectives and what you want to achieve through attribution modeling. It could be increasing conversions, optimizing marketing spend, or improving ROI.

3. Collect Data

- Integrate Analytics Tools: Ensure you have integrated analytics tools like Google Analytics, Adobe Analytics, or custom attribution software to collect data on user interactions across marketing channels.

- Data Quality: Verify that your data is accurate, complete, and up to date. Any inconsistencies can lead to incorrect attribution results.

4. Choose the Right Attribution Model

- Model Selection: Depending on your business and objectives, select the most suitable attribution model. Consider using models like algorithmic attribution if you have access to robust data and tools.

- Custom Models: Some analytics platforms allow you to create custom attribution models tailored to your unique business needs.

5. Analyze Attribution Data

- Review Reports: Use your analytics platform to generate attribution reports. These reports will show you how different channels and touchpoints contribute to conversions.

- Channel Performance: Analyze how each marketing channel performs along the customer journey. Understand which channels are more influential at different stages.

- Cross-Device Attribution: If relevant to your business, consider cross-device attribution to track how users switch between devices before converting.

6. Allocate Resources Effectively

- Budget Allocation: Armed with attribution insights, adjust your marketing budget allocation. Allocate more resources to channels that contribute significantly to conversions.

- Optimize Campaigns: Optimize your marketing campaigns based on the attribution data. Focus on improving the performance of channels and touchpoints that have a high impact on conversions.

7. Test and Iterate

- A/B Testing: Conduct A/B tests to validate the insights gained from your attribution model. Test different strategies and measure their impact on conversions.

- Continuous Improvement: Attribution modeling is an ongoing process. Continuously refine your models and strategies as customer behavior and market dynamics change.

8. Educate Your Team

- Training: Ensure your marketing team is well-versed in attribution modeling concepts and understands how to use attribution insights for decision-making.

9. Monitor and Report

- Regular Monitoring: Set up a schedule for regular monitoring of attribution reports. Track changes in performance and adjust strategies accordingly.

- Reporting: Provide clear and concise attribution reports to stakeholders and decision-makers in your organization to keep everyone informed.

10. Consider Attribution Software

- Third-Party Solutions: Explore third-party attribution software solutions that offer features and automation for more complex attribution modeling.

Implementing attribution models empowers you to make data-driven decisions and allocate marketing resources where they have the most impact. It helps you optimize your marketing strategies for maximum efficiency and effectiveness in a constantly evolving digital landscape.

III. Conversion Rate Optimization (CRO)

Master CRO techniques to maximize the impact of your marketing efforts. Conduct A/B tests, multivariate tests, and user behavior analysis to optimize conversion paths.

Mastering Conversion Rate Optimization (CRO) techniques is crucial for new entrepreneurs to maximize the impact of their marketing efforts and improve the conversion rates of their websites or landing pages. Here's a step-by-step guide on how to do this:

1. Understand the Basics

- Learn the Fundamentals: Begin by gaining a solid understanding of CRO principles, including the conversion funnel, user experience (UX) design, and the importance of data-driven decisions.

2. Define Your Conversion Goals

- Specific Objectives: Clearly define the actions you want users to take on your website, such as making a purchase, filling out a contact form, or subscribing to a newsletter.

3. Conduct User Behavior Analysis

- Heatmaps: Use heatmap tools like Hotjar or Crazy Egg to visualize how users interact with your website. Heatmaps show where users click, move their cursors, and spend the most time.

- Session Recordings: Record user sessions to gain insights into how individual users navigate your site. Identify pain points and areas where users drop off.

- Conversion Funnels: Set up conversion funnels in Google Analytics or similar tools to track the steps users take before converting. Identify where users abandon the funnel.

4. A/B Testing

- Hypothesis Development: Formulate hypotheses about elements on your website that may impact conversions. For example, changing the color of a call-to-action (CTA) button could increase clicks.

- Test Variations: Create two or more versions (A and B) of the webpage with different elements. Make sure only one variable is changed at a time to isolate its impact.

- Randomized Testing: Use A/B testing software like Optimizely, VWO (Visual Website Optimizer), or Google Optimize to conduct randomized tests on your live site.

- Statistical Significance: Ensure you gather a sufficient sample size and run tests until they reach statistical significance. Tools often provide statistical analysis to determine the winning variation.

5. Multivariate Testing

- Testing: Once you're comfortable with A/B testing, consider multivariate testing. This involves testing multiple variations of multiple elements on a page simultaneously.

- Complex Hypotheses: Multivariate tests are suitable for more complex hypotheses that involve changing several page elements at once.

- Resource Intensive: Keep in mind that multivariate testing requires a larger sample size and may take longer to yield results.

6. User Surveys and Feedback

- User Surveys: Use tools like SurveyMonkey or Google Forms to gather user feedback. Ask questions about their experience, pain points, and suggestions for improvement.

- On-Site Feedback: Implement on-site feedback tools that allow users to provide input directly on your website.

7. Continuously Iterate

- Continuous Improvement: CRO is an ongoing process. Regularly review and analyze the results of your tests and user behavior data. Implement changes based on what you learn.

- Iterative Testing: Continue testing and optimizing different elements of your website. Even small improvements can have a significant impact over time.

8. User-Centric Design

- Mobile Optimization: Ensure that your website is responsive and optimized for mobile devices, as an increasing number of users access websites on smartphones and tablets.

- User-Centered Design: Design your website with a focus on the user experience. Make navigation intuitive, content easily readable, and CTAs (call-to-action) prominent.

9. Seek Expert Advice

- If you're new to CRO or your website is complex or all of this information is overwhelming (and it is!) consider hiring CRO experts or agencies with experience in optimizing conversion paths. I always hire an agency. They are the most up to date with the latest advancements and things change rapidly in this space. If you are allocating your budgets, I highly recommend prioritizing the outsourcing of this work.

10. Monitor Metrics

- Key Metrics: Keep an eye on key performance indicators (KPIs) related to conversions, such as conversion rate, bounce rate, click-through rate, and average session duration.

By mastering CRO techniques and conducting A/B tests, multivariate tests, and user behavior analysis, you can optimize conversion paths on your website, enhance the user experience, and ultimately achieve higher conversion rates and improved ROI on your marketing efforts. CRO is a continuous process of refinement, so be prepared to adapt and iterate based on data-driven insights.

Section 7: Mastering Traditional Marketing Techniques

Embracing traditional marketing techniques, alongside digital strategies, is crucial for new entrepreneurs for several compelling reasons:

- Broader Audience Reach: Traditional marketing methods such as print ads, radio, TV commercials, and direct mail can reach a diverse and often older audience that might not be as active online. By using both traditional and digital approaches, you can maximize your reach and target various demographic groups.

- Establishing Credibility: Traditional marketing methods, especially when combined with digital efforts, can help establish your brand's credibility and legitimacy. Being featured in reputable print publications, for example, can boost your reputation and build trust with potential customers.

- Local and Regional Focus: If your business primarily serves a local or regional market, traditional marketing can be highly effective. Local newspaper ads, community events, and billboards can help you connect with your target audience in a tangible way.

- Tangible Brand Presence: Traditional marketing provides a tangible brand presence that digital marketing alone cannot replicate. People can touch, see, or hear your marketing materials, creating a lasting impression.

- Multichannel Marketing: Successful marketing often involves a multichannel approach. By combining traditional and digital strategies, you can reinforce your brand message and reach consumers through various touchpoints, increasing the likelihood of conversion.

- Cultural and Generational Diversity: Different generations may respond better to different marketing channels. Traditional methods can be more effective in targeting older demographics, while digital strategies may resonate with younger generations. Utilizing both approaches ensures that you cover a wide spectrum of potential customers.

- Effective Storytelling: Traditional marketing, such as television and radio ads, allows for creative and emotive storytelling. These mediums can convey your brand's story, values, and message in a compelling way that resonates with your audience on an emotional level.

- Event Marketing: Traditional marketing methods like trade shows, exhibitions, and in-person events offer opportunities for direct interaction with potential customers. These events can be highly effective for B2B businesses and industries where face-to-face relationships matter.

- Building Brand Recognition: Consistency across traditional and digital channels helps build brand recognition. When customers encounter your brand through various mediums, it reinforces your presence and makes your brand more memorable.

- Market Saturation: In some industries or regions, digital advertising can be highly competitive and saturated.

Traditional methods can provide an alternative way to stand out and capture the attention of potential customers.

- Complementary Strategies: Traditional and digital marketing methods can complement each other. For instance, a TV commercial can drive traffic to your website, where customers can learn more about your products or services and make a purchase.

- Market Research and Testing: Traditional marketing efforts can serve as a valuable source of market research. By analyzing the response to different traditional campaigns, you can gather insights that inform your overall marketing strategy.

Traditional Marketing Techniques Explained

Traditional marketing techniques encompass a wide range of strategies and methods that have been used for decades to promote products, services, or brands. These techniques typically rely on offline channels to reach and engage with the target audience. Here are some key traditional marketing techniques and what they can achieve, including public relations campaigns:

1. Print Advertising

- Types: Print advertising includes newspaper ads, magazine ads, brochures, flyers, and posters.

- Achievements: Print advertising can help raise brand awareness, promote special offers or events, and target specific geographic areas or demographics.

2. Television Advertising

- Types: Television commercials can be broadcast on network or cable TV, as well as local channels.

- Achievements: TV ads can reach a wide audience, create memorable brand experiences, and convey complex messages through visuals and audio.

3. Radio Advertising

- Types: Radio ads are broadcast over AM/FM stations or digital radio platforms.

- Achievements: Radio ads are effective for delivering short, catchy messages and can reach a local or regional audience effectively.

4. Direct Mail Marketing

- Types: Direct mail includes postcards, catalogs, letters, and promotional materials sent via postal mail.

- Achievements: Direct mail can target specific households, generate leads, and provide tangible marketing materials.

5. Outdoor Advertising

- Types: Outdoor ads comprise billboards, transit ads (on buses and subways), and signage on buildings.

- Achievements: Outdoor ads are excellent for creating brand visibility in high-traffic areas and reaching a local audience.

6. Event Marketing

- Types: Event marketing includes sponsoring or participating in trade shows, exhibitions, conferences, and community events.

- Achievements: Event marketing allows for in-person engagement, networking, and showcasing products or services to a targeted audience.

7. Public Relations (PR) Campaigns

- Types: PR campaigns involve building relationships with media, writing press releases, hosting press conferences, and managing crisis communication.

- Achievements: PR campaigns can enhance brand reputation, generate positive media coverage, address public concerns, and manage the public perception of the business.

8. Sponsorships and Partnerships

- Types: Businesses can sponsor local events, sports teams, or charitable causes, or form partnerships and collaborate with complementary brands.

- Achievements: Sponsorships and partnerships can align your brand with positive associations, increase visibility, and create goodwill in the community.

9. Telemarketing

- Types: Telemarketing involves making phone calls to potential customers to promote products or services.

- Achievements: Telemarketing can generate leads, conduct surveys, and provide personalized interactions with potential customers.

10. Public Speaking and Seminars

- Types: Public speaking engagements and seminars allow business leaders to share expertise and insights.

- Achievements: Speaking engagements can position you as an industry authority, build trust, and attract potential clients or partners.

11. Trade Shows and Exhibitions

- Types: Participating in industry-specific trade shows and exhibitions allows businesses to showcase products and services.

- Achievements: Trade shows offer opportunities for networking, lead generation, and product demonstrations.

12. Magazine Articles and Editorials

- Types: Getting featured in industry magazines or newspapers can provide expert insights, interviews, or profiles.

- Achievements: Magazine features can enhance brand authority and reach a targeted readership.

Traditional marketing techniques, including public relations campaigns, are still valuable for many businesses. They offer a chance to reach audiences through offline channels and establish credibility, especially when integrated with digital marketing efforts. Entrepreneurs should carefully select the techniques that align with their target audience, industry, and marketing objectives to create a well-rounded marketing strategy.

Chapter 7:
Funding Your Dreams

Section 1: Traditional vs. Alternative Funding

Funding is the lifeblood of your business. I'll compare traditional funding sources like bank loans with alternative options like crowdfunding and angel investors. Discover how to build relationships with potential investors and secure the capital you need.

The choices you make in this realm can significantly impact your entrepreneurial journey. In this chapter, we will dissect the world of funding, comparing traditional sources, such as bank loans, with alternative options, including crowdfunding and angel investors. You'll also learn the art of building meaningful relationships with potential investors to secure the capital you need to bring your business dreams to life.

Traditional Funding Avenues

1. Bank Loans

Dive deep into the world of bank loans, exploring the intricacies of securing loans, from preparing a solid business plan and financial statements to understanding different types of loans, including term loans, lines of credit, and Small Business Administration (SBA) loans.

Bank loans are a common form of financing that new entrepreneurs can utilize to start or grow their businesses. These loans involve borrowing money from a bank or financial institution with the agreement to repay the borrowed amount, plus interest, over a specified period. Securing a bank loan involves several intricacies:

I. Preparation

Business Plan: A solid business plan is crucial when seeking a bank loan. It should outline your business concept, market analysis, financial projections, and repayment strategy. A well-structured plan demonstrates your commitment and understanding of your business.

Here's a simple, mocked-up business plan for you to model yours off (again, feel free to use this as a template for yours).

M Label—a luxury, sustainable fashion label

Business Plan for M Label

1. Executive Summary:

- Business Name: M Label

- Founder: Danielle Corby

- Business Concept: M Label is a high-end fashion label specializing in sustainable, luxury clothing and accessories. Our commitment to eco-conscious practices and exquisite design sets us apart.

- Market Opportunity: The fashion industry is evolving towards sustainability, with consumers seeking both luxury and ethical fashion options.

2. Business Concept:

- Description: M Label creates exclusive, sustainable fashion collections for women and men, blending elegance with eco-friendliness. Our products are crafted using ethically sourced materials and artisanal techniques.

- Mission Statement: Our mission is to redefine luxury fashion by offering impeccably designed, sustainable clothing that reflects our values of quality, responsibility, and style.

3. Market Analysis:

- Market Research: Extensive research reveals a growing demand for sustainable luxury fashion among discerning consumers. We aim to cater to individuals who seek exclusive, eco-conscious attire.

- Competitive Analysis: Key competitors include established luxury fashion brands with limited sustainable offerings.

4. Marketing Strategy:

- Target Market: Our target audience comprises affluent consumers who prioritize sustainability and luxury. We aim to build a loyal clientele through exquisite design and ethical values.

- Value Proposition: M Label offers the finest in sustainable luxury fashion, combining opulence, comfort, and ethical production.

- Marketing Plan: Our strategy includes high-end fashion events, collaborations with eco-conscious influencers, and a strong online presence.

5. Operations and Management:

- Team: Our team includes top-tier fashion designers, skilled artisans, and a marketing and sales team with a passion for luxury fashion.

- Location: Our design and administrative offices are based in Sydney, while production takes place in artisanal workshops around the world.

- Production/Service Process: We source the finest sustainable materials, collaborate with artisans, and maintain meticulous quality control.

6. Financial Projections: (This is VERY basic and is just designed to give you a quick grasp of the kind of detail required.) As I have said in many sections of this book, getting professional help with accounting is crucial—it's the life force of your business!

Startup Costs:

- Equipment and Supplies: $200,000

- Marketing and Branding: $150,000

- Initial Inventory: $300,000

- Legal and Licensing: $50,000

- Working Capital: $200,000

Sales Forecast:

- Year 1: $1,000,000

- Year 2: $1,200,000 (20% YoY Growth)

- Year 3: $1,440,000 (20% YoY Growth)

Expense Budget (Monthly):

- Rent and Utilities: $10,000

- Marketing and Advertising: $20,000

- Salaries and Wages: $60,000

- Materials and Production: $70,000

- General and Administrative: $20,000

Profit and Loss Statement (Year 1):

Category	Amount ($)
Total Revenue	$1,000,000
Cost of Goods Sold (COGS)	$300,000
Gross Profit	$700,000
Operating Expenses	$720,000
Net Profit Before Tax	($20,000)

Assumptions for Financial Projections:

- Sales growth assumes successful brand launch and marketing efforts.

- COGS is based on industry averages for luxury sustainable fashion.

- Monthly expenses are estimated based on anticipated costs.

- Working capital is allocated to cover operational needs.

7. Funding Request:

- Amount Needed: We are seeking $500,000 in capital to cover startup costs, initial inventory, and working capital.

- Use of Funds: Funds will be used for equipment, marketing, inventory, and operational expenses.

- Repayment Strategy: We propose a 5-year term loan with a 10% interest rate, monthly repayments, and a personal guarantee.

8. Appendix:

- Supporting Documents: Include market research findings, financial projections, and resumes of key team members.

9. Conclusion:

Call to Action: We invite potential investors to discuss our business plan further and explore a partnership with M Label.

This mock-up business plan outlines the concept for M Label, provides insights into the market analysis, financial projections, and a funding request. The plan demonstrates the feasibility of achieving a $1 million turnover in the first year with a 20% year-on-year growth rate. Customize this plan with your specific details to present a compelling case for investors or lenders.

Financial Statements

Prepare financial statements, including a balance sheet, income statement, and cash flow statement. These documents provide a snapshot of your business's financial health and ability to repay the loan.

1. Balance Sheet in Excel:

- Open a new Excel spreadsheet.

- In the first column (Column A), list your assets under "ASSETS" and your liabilities under "LIABILITIES."

- In the second column (Column B), input the corresponding amounts.

- Calculate "Total Assets" by summing the values in Column A for assets.

- Calculate "Total Liabilities" by summing the values in Column B for liabilities.

- Calculate "Owner's Equity" as Total Assets minus Total Liabilities.

2. Income Statement (Profit and Loss Statement) in Excel:

- Open a new Excel spreadsheet.

- Create a table with the following columns: "Revenue," "Cost of Goods Sold (COGS)," "Gross Profit," "Operating Expenses," and "Net Profit (Loss)."

- Input your revenue, COGS, and operating expenses in the corresponding columns.

- Calculate "Gross Profit" as Revenue minus COGS.

- Calculate "Net Profit (Loss)" as Gross Profit minus Operating Expenses

3. Cash Flow Statement in Excel:

- Open a new Excel spreadsheet.

- Create a table with the following columns: "Operating Activities," "Investing Activities," "Financing Activities," "Net Increase (Decrease) in Cash," "Beginning Cash Balance," and "Ending Cash Balance."

- Input the cash flows for operating, investing, and financing activities in the corresponding columns.

- Calculate "Net Increase (Decrease) in Cash" as the sum of all cash flows.

- Calculate "Ending Cash Balance" as "Beginning Cash Balance" plus "Net Increase (Decrease) in Cash."

Once you've inputted the data and formulas, Excel will automatically calculate the totals and subtotals for you. You can then save the Excel file for your reference and reporting. I always get an experienced CFO (Chief Financial Officer) or Accountant to help me prepare mine and I highly recommend that you do this, too. As with the digital marketing outsourcing, this is a highly specialized field and as it's the life blood of your business, it is crucial that you get this information right before proceeding.

II. Types of Bank Loans

- Term Loans: Term loans are the most common type of bank loan. They provide a lump sum amount upfront, which is repaid in regular installments over a predetermined period, typically with a fixed interest rate. Term loans are often used for specific purposes, such as buying equipment or expanding operations.

- Lines of Credit: A line of credit allows you to borrow funds up to a predefined limit as needed. You only pay interest on the amount borrowed, making it a flexible option for managing short-term expenses or cash flow gaps. Be careful: I once used a home loan line of credit to fund some business expenses for a business that failed—ouch!

- Small Business Administration (SBA) Loans: SBA loans are guaranteed by the U.S. Small Business Administration. They offer favorable terms and lower interest rates but involve a more extensive application process. SBA loans come in various forms, including 7(a) loans for general business needs and 504 loans for real estate and equipment financing.

III. Creditworthiness

- Personal Credit Score: Banks often consider your personal credit score when evaluating your loan application. A strong credit score can increase your chances of approval and secure better terms.

- Business Credit: If your business has a credit history, maintain a positive credit record by paying bills on time and managing debts responsibly.

IV. Collateral

- Secured Loans: Some bank loans may require collateral, such as real estate, equipment, or inventory, to secure the loan. If you default on the loan, the bank can seize the collateral.

- Unsecured Loans: Unsecured loans do not require collateral but may have higher interest rates and stricter qualification criteria.

V. Down Payment

- Equity Injection: Banks often expect entrepreneurs to contribute a down payment or equity injection. This demonstrates your commitment to the business and reduces the bank's risk. But don't forget that if you take this option, and your business fails, you will be personally on the hook like I was.

VI. Loan Terms and Interest Rates

- Fixed vs. Variable Rates: Determine whether you prefer a fixed interest rate, which remains constant throughout the loan term, or a variable rate that may change with market fluctuations.

- Loan Term: The loan term dictates how long you have to repay the loan. Longer terms can result in lower monthly payments but may accrue more interest.

VII. Application Process

- Choose a Lender: Research and select a bank or financial institution that specializes in business loans and suits your needs.

- Application Submission: Complete the loan application, including all required documentation and financial statements.

- Evaluation: The lender reviews your application, credit history, and financial documents. They may request additional information or clarification.

- Approval: If approved, you'll receive a loan offer outlining the terms and conditions. Carefully review the offer and ensure you understand all terms before accepting.

- Loan Disbursement: Once accepted, the bank disburses the loan amount to your business account, and you can start using the funds for your intended purpose.

- Repayment: Make timely payments according to the agreed-upon schedule, including principal and interest.

Securing a bank loan requires careful planning, preparation, and an understanding of the various loan options available. Entrepreneurs should choose the type of loan that best suits their business needs, maintain good credit, and present a well-structured business plan to increase their chances of approval. Consulting with a financial advisor or business consultant can also provide valuable guidance during the loan application process.

2. Venture Capital

Understand the venture capital landscape, from identifying the right venture capitalists for your business to preparing a compelling pitch deck and negotiating terms. Here we will delve into topics like valuation and equity distribution.

I. Understanding the Venture Capital Landscape

1. Introduction to Venture Capital (VC)

Venture capital involves investing in startups or early-stage companies with high growth potential. VCs provide funding in exchange for equity ownership. Understanding the role of VCs is crucial to align your business goals.

2. Types of Venture Capital

Different stages of VC funding:

- Seed stage: Funding for product development and market research.

- Early-stage: Financing for business growth and scaling.

- Growth-stage: Capital for expansion into new markets or product lines.

Industry-Focused VC Firms: Some VC firms specialize in specific industries like technology, healthcare, or clean energy. Choose a VC aligned with your business sector and stage.

3. Identifying the Right VC Firm

Research and due diligence:

- Study the portfolio of VC firms to see if they have invested in companies similar to yours.

- Seek out firms with a history of successful exits.

- Evaluate the reputation and track record of the VC firm.

Compatibility:

- Ensure the VC's investment thesis aligns with your business goals and values.

II. Preparing for VC Funding

1. Business Plan and Pitch Deck

- Crafting a Compelling Business Plan: As we've covered in previous chapters, outline your business concept, target market, competitive analysis, and financial projections.

- Building a Comprehensive Pitch Deck: Create a visually appealing presentation with key information, including your problem statement, solution, market opportunity, team, financials, and exit strategy.

2. Financial Projections

Creating realistic financial models:

- Develop detailed financial projections, including income statements, balance sheets, and cash flow statements.

- Show a clear path to profitability.

- Highlight the scalability of your business model.

3. Valuation and Equity

Understanding startup valuation methods:

- Discounted Cash Flow (DCF), Market Comparables, and Risk-Adjusted Return methods.

- Balancing valuation expectations with equity dilution: Be prepared to negotiate the percentage of equity you're willing to exchange for funding.

4. Term Sheet Preparation

- Key Terms and Clauses: Familiarize yourself with common terms like valuation, equity stake, board seats, liquidation preferences, and anti-dilution provisions.

- Negotiation Strategies: Seek legal counsel or advisors with expertise in VC negotiations.

III. Navigating the VC Funding Process

1. Networking and Relationship Building

- Building Connections with VC Firms: Attend industry events, pitch competitions, and networking functions to establish relationships with potential investors.

- Leveraging Industry Networks: Utilize mentorship programs, accelerators, and business associations to expand your network.

2. Pitching to VCs

- Crafting a Captivating Pitch Presentation: Develop a compelling narrative that showcases your unique value proposition, market opportunity, and team.

- Pitching to Potential Investors: Practice your pitch with advisors or mentors to refine your delivery.

3. Due Diligence

- VC's Evaluation of Your Business: Be prepared for in-depth scrutiny of your business model, financials, legal documents, and team.

- Address any concerns proactively.

4. Negotiating Terms

- Term Sheet Negotiation: Engage in constructive discussions about terms, seeking a win-win outcome.

- Understand the implications of each term on your business's future.

5. Closing the Deal

- Finalizing the Funding Round: Once both parties agree on terms, work with legal counsel to complete the necessary documentation.

- Comply with legal and regulatory requirements.

IV. Post-Investment Management

1. Managing Investor Relations

- Maintaining Communication with VCs: Keep your investors informed about significant developments and challenges.

- Establish regular reporting mechanisms.

- You should make a mutually agreeable time to check in with them—be it weekly, fortnightly, or monthly. Typically, if they want weekly check-ins, they are going to be very hands-on. This can be both a good or a bad thing and most entrepreneurs would say that being hands-on will take you away from the business when you're that focused on investor relations. This goes for all types of funding.

2. Effective Use of Funds

- Utilizing capital for growth and scaling: Execute your business plan and use funds strategically to achieve key milestones.

- Monitor expenses closely.

3. Governance and Reporting

- Adhering to agreed-upon governance structures: Follow the governance framework outlined in your term sheet.

- Hold regular board meetings and adhere to reporting requirements.

4. Preparing for Future Funding Rounds:

- Planning for Follow-on Financing: Strategically position your company for subsequent rounds of funding.

- Showcase progress achieved since the last round.

V. Exit Strategies

1. Preparing for Exit

- Different Exit Options: Explore various exit strategies, such as an Initial Public Offering (IPO), acquisition, or secondary sale.

- Timing Considerations: Evaluate the right time to exit based on market conditions and business growth.

2. Maximizing Valuation

- Strategies For Increasing Company Value: Implement measures to boost your company's valuation before exiting. This could include introducing new revenue streams to creating competitive tension in the market.

- Evaluate offers to ensure they align with your valuation expectations. Again, external input from your legal counsel or lawyer(s) and accountants will be of significant value in this process. I wouldn't proceed without their strategic and expert input.

3. Exit Negotiations

- Negotiating the Terms of the Exit: Engage in negotiations with potential buyers or market regulators. Again, I would engage with the experts to represent you and your interests.

- Secure the best possible terms for your exit.

VI. Case Studies and Real-World Insights

1. Analyzing Successful VC Stories: Study case studies of successful startups and their VC journeys to understand what worked for them.

2. Learning from Failures: Review examples of startups that faced challenges or rejection by VCs to identify common pitfalls. Tamara Mellon, the Founder of Jimmy Choo, has an excellent book called *In My Shoes* that details her trials and tribulations on her VC journey. I highly recommend you read this if you're heading down this path.

3. Guest Speaker Sessions: Invite successful entrepreneurs and venture capitalists to share their experiences and insights.

VII. Continuous Learning and Adaptation

1. Staying Informed: Keep up with evolving VC trends by regularly reading industry publications and attending conferences.

2. Adapting to Feedback: Continuously improve your business plan and strategy based on feedback received during the funding process.

This comprehensive guide provides a detailed roadmap for new entrepreneurs navigating the venture capital landscape, from initial preparation to post-investment management and exit strategies, with an emphasis on the value of expert representation, continuous learning and adaptation.

3. Business Grants

Explore the realm of business grants, including government grants and private foundation grants. Learn how to identify grant opportunities, craft winning grant proposals, and navigate the application process.

I. Understanding Business Grants

1. Introduction to Business Grants

Business grants are funds awarded to businesses and entrepreneurs to support specific projects or initiatives. They do not require repayment, unlike loans.

2. Types of Business Grants

- Government Grants: Offered by federal, state, or local government agencies to promote economic development, innovation, and job creation.

- Private Foundation Grants: Provided by non-profit organizations, private foundations, and corporate entities with a philanthropic mission.

II. Identifying Grant Opportunities

1. Research and Due Diligence

- Identify relevant grant programs by conducting research online, through government websites, and grant databases.

- Look for grants aligned with your industry, business stage, and project goals.

2. Eligibility Criteria

- Review the eligibility requirements, including geographical restrictions, business size, and project focus.

- Ensure your business meets all criteria before proceeding with an application.

3. Networking and Relationships

- Attend grant-related events, workshops, and seminars to network with grant providers and other entrepreneurs.

- Establish connections within the grant community for insights and opportunities.

III. Crafting a Winning Grant Proposal

1. Proposal Structure

- Create a clear and concise proposal that includes an executive summary, project description, budget, timeline, and impact assessment.

2. Demonstrating Need and Purpose

- Clearly outline why your project is essential and how it addresses a specific need or problem.

- Emphasize the project's alignment with the grantor's mission or objectives.

3. Project Plan and Budget

- Detail the project plan, including objectives, methods, milestones, and deliverables.

- Prepare a comprehensive budget that breaks down costs and demonstrates financial responsibility.

4. Measurable Outcomes

- Define specific, measurable, achievable, relevant, and time-bound (SMART) objectives.

- Explain how success will be measured and evaluated.

5. Impact and Sustainability:

- Highlight the potential positive impact of your project on the community, industry, or economy.

- Discuss how the project will be sustained beyond the grant period.

IV. Navigating the Application Process

1. Application Requirements

- Carefully review the grant application guidelines, formatting requirements, and submission deadlines.

- Gather all necessary documents, including business plans, financial statements, and letters of support.

2. Grant Writing Tips

- Get an experienced grant writer to work on this for you. If you can afford it, of course. Otherwise, write persuasively and concisely, focusing on the most compelling aspects of your proposal.

- Proofread and edit your application to ensure clarity and professionalism.

3. Application Submission

- Submit your grant application following the specified process, whether online, by mail, or in person.

- Retain copies of all submitted materials for your records.

4. Follow-Up and Communication

- Be prepared for potential follow-up questions or requests for additional information.

- Maintain open communication with grant providers and respond promptly to inquiries.

V. Post-Grant Management

1. Compliance and Reporting

- Comply with grant requirements, including project implementation, financial reporting, and documentation.

- Meet reporting deadlines and provide accurate progress updates.

2. Acknowledgment and Recognition

- Acknowledge the grantor's support in your project's publicity and communications.

- Show appreciation by attending grant-related events and recognizing their contribution.

3. Evaluation and Impact Assessment

- Continuously assess the project's progress and impact on the intended beneficiaries.

- Share results and success stories with the grant provider and the public.

4. Building Relationships

- Cultivate ongoing relationships with grant providers, as they may offer additional funding opportunities in the future.

- Attend grant-related events and engage with the grant community.

Navigating the realm of business grants requires thorough research, careful preparation, and effective communication. By identifying the right opportunities, crafting compelling proposals, and following through with responsible post-grant management, you can increase your chances of securing valuable funding for your projects and initiatives.

Alternative Funding Avenues

1. Crowdfunding

Learn how to master the art of crowdfunding, including running successful Kickstarter or Indiegogo campaigns. Here I will explain crowdfunding strategies, such as creating compelling video pitches, setting achievable funding goals, and effectively promoting your campaign.

I. Understanding Crowdfunding

1. Introduction to Crowdfunding: Crowdfunding is a method of raising funds for a project or business by collecting small contributions from a large number of people, typically online.

2. Crowdfunding Platforms: Platforms like Kickstarter and Indiegogo provide a space to showcase your project and collect funds from backers.

II. Preparing for a Crowdfunding Campaign

1. Project Planning

- Immerse yourself in the world of Crowdfunding Campaigns. Look at ones that have worked and ones that have tanked. This will be a good introduction into finding out if it's for you. Develop a comprehensive project plan, including a clear description of your idea, its value proposition, and the problem it solves.

2. Setting Funding Goals

- Determine the minimum amount required to bring your project to life.

- Be realistic and transparent about how funds will be used.

3. Building a Crowd

- Establish a strong online presence through social media, a website, and email marketing.

- Start engaging with potential backers before launching your campaign.

III. Crafting a Compelling Crowdfunding Campaign

1. Creating a Compelling Video Pitch

- Develop an engaging video that tells your story, showcases your product or idea, and connects with potential backers emotionally.

- Highlight the benefits and impact of your project (search for other campaigns that are or have already raised substantial funds and watch how they have created compelling video strategies to give you ideas).

2. Crafting an Irresistible Campaign Page

- Write a persuasive campaign description that addresses the problem your project solves and explains why backers should support it.

- Use high-quality images and graphics to visually represent your idea.

3. Rewards and Perks

- Offer attractive and meaningful rewards to backers at different contribution levels.

- Make sure the rewards align with the project and offer good value.

IV. Launching and Running the Campaign

1. Timing and Duration

- Choose the right time to launch your campaign, considering seasonal trends and holidays.

- Typically, campaigns run for 30–45 days.

2. Promotion and Outreach

- Utilize social media, email marketing, and press releases to promote your campaign.

- Engage with your backers and respond promptly to comments and questions.

3. Updates and Milestones

- Regularly update your backers on campaign progress, achievements, and any changes.

- Celebrate milestones and share your excitement.

V. Managing Crowdfunding Success

1. Fulfillment and Delivery

- Plan for how you will fulfill rewards and deliver products to backers.

- Communicate clearly about delivery timelines.

2. Gratitude and Appreciation

- Show appreciation to your backers with personalized thank-you messages.

- Acknowledge their role in making your project a reality.

3. Post-Campaign Engagement

- Continue engaging with your backers and provide updates on project developments.

- Consider offering post-campaign perks or exclusive content.

VI. Crowdfunding Strategies

1. Stretch Goals

- Introduce stretch goals to encourage backers to increase their pledges.

- Stretch goals offer additional features or upgrades as incentives.

2. Cross-Promotion

- Collaborate with other campaigns or creators for cross-promotion.

- Tap into their audiences to expand your reach.

3. Media and PR

- Work with media outlets and bloggers to get press coverage.

- Craft compelling press releases and reach out to journalists.

4. Backer Engagement

- Create a sense of community among your backers by involving them in decisions, polls, or exclusive content.

- Encourage backers to share your campaign within their networks.

Running a successful crowdfunding campaign requires careful planning, engaging storytelling, and effective promotion. Strategies such as stretch goals, cross-promotion, and media outreach can help maximize your campaign's reach and impact. By nurturing relationships with backers and delivering on promises, you can build a loyal community around your project.

2. Angel Investors

Let's now explore the world of angel investors, from identifying potential angel investors to preparing a captivating investor pitch. Understand the nuances of angel investing, including terms, equity, and due diligence. This is my preferred path to funding.

I. Understanding Angel Investors

1. Introduction to Angel Investors

Angel investors are affluent individuals who provide capital to startups or early-stage companies in exchange for equity ownership.

2. Role of Angel Investors

Angel investors play a pivotal role in bridging the funding gap for entrepreneurs, offering financial support and mentorship.

II. Identifying Potential Angel Investors

1. Networking and Events

Attend industry events, networking gatherings, and pitch competitions to connect with potential angel investors. Always be on the lookout for potential Angels and cultivate these relationships even when you're not working on a startup. You never know when a contact will come in handy.

2. Angel Investor Groups

Research local angel investor groups or networks that specialize in supporting startups.

3. Online Platforms

Utilize online platforms like AngelList or Gust to identify and connect with angel investors interested in your industry.

III. Preparing a Captivating Investor Pitch

1. Crafting a Compelling Pitch Deck

- Develop a well-structured pitch deck that covers your business concept, market opportunity, team, financials, and growth strategy. We've already covered most of this in previous chapters, so you should have this information at the ready.

2. Addressing Key Questions

- Anticipate and address potential questions or concerns angel investors may have.

3. Elevator Pitch

Create a concise and engaging elevator pitch that communicates your business idea in a minute or less.

I love an elevator pitch! They are so effective—no one has time anymore to hear a long-form version of your offering. Here are some tips on crafting yours:

- Start with a Hook: Begin your pitch with a concise and attention-grabbing hook. This can be a compelling question, a surprising fact, or a bold statement related to your business.

- Explain the Problem: Clearly articulate the problem or pain point that your business addresses. Make it relatable and show empathy for the audience's pain.

- Present Your Solution: Describe your business idea or product and how it solves the problem. Focus on the benefits and unique selling points that set your solution apart.

- Highlight Key Benefits: Highlight the main benefits or advantages of your business. Explain why your solution is valuable and what sets it apart from the competition.

- Share Your Unique Selling Proposition (USP): Emphasize what makes your business unique or different from others in the market. This could be a patented technology, a unique approach, or a special feature.

- Provide Social Proof: If applicable, mention any notable achievements, partnerships, or customer testimonials that lend credibility to your business.

- Call to Action: Conclude your pitch with a clear and compelling call to action. What do you want the listener to do next? Whether it's scheduling a meeting, trying your product, or investing, be specific.

- Practice and Refine: Practice your elevator pitch until it flows naturally and is well within the one-minute time frame. Rehearse it with friends or mentors to get feedback and refine it further.

Example of an Engaging Elevator Pitch:

Imagine you're the founder of a tech startup that has developed a cutting-edge app for remote project management. Here's how you could craft your elevator pitch:

- Start with a Hook: "Do you ever feel like managing remote projects is like herding cats?"

- Explain the Problem: "In today's increasingly remote and distributed work environments, project management has become more challenging than ever. Teams are scattered, communication is fragmented, and deadlines often slip through the cracks."

- Present Your Solution: "That's where our app, 'ProjectFlow,' comes in. It's a revolutionary project management tool designed specifically for remote teams. With ProjectFlow, you can seamlessly collaborate, track tasks, and meet deadlines, no matter where your team members are located."

- Highlight Key Benefits: "What sets us apart is our intuitive user interface and real-time analytics. Our app not only simplifies project management but also provides valuable insights to optimize team performance and productivity."

- Share Your USP: "Unlike other project management tools, ProjectFlow was built from the ground up for remote work, making it uniquely tailored to the challenges of today's business landscape."

- Provide Social Proof: "We've already helped companies like [mention a well-known client] achieve a 20% increase in project efficiency and a 30% reduction in missed deadlines."

- Call to Action: "I'd love to show you a quick demo of ProjectFlow and discuss how it could streamline project management for your team. Can we schedule a brief call this week?"

Remember, the key to a successful elevator pitch is to be concise, compelling, and focused on the most important aspects of your business. Tailor your pitch to your audience and practice it until it feels natural and engaging.

IV. Nuances of Angel Investing

1. Terms and Agreements

- Angel investors typically negotiate terms, which may include valuation, equity ownership, board seats, and anti-dilution clauses.

2. Equity Ownership

- Be prepared to discuss and negotiate the percentage of equity you're willing to exchange for investment.

3. Due Diligence

- Angel investors conduct due diligence to assess the viability and potential risks of your business.

- Prepare for questions related to your business model, market research, financial projections, and competitive landscape.

4. Angel Investor Involvement

- Some angel investors take an active role in mentoring and advising startups.

- Discuss expectations regarding their involvement in your business.

V. Investor Pitch Meeting

1. Preparation: Practice your pitch multiple times and be ready to answer questions confidently.

2. Pitch Meeting: During the meeting, focus on conveying your passion for the business, your understanding of the market, and your vision for growth.

3. Building Rapport: Build a positive and professional relationship with potential investors, demonstrating your commitment and integrity.

VI. Post-Investment Management

1. Reporting and Communication

- Keep angel investors informed about your progress, achievements, and challenges.

- Provide regular updates on financial performance and milestones.

2. Advisory Role

- Leverage the expertise and advice of angel investors to make informed business decisions. Putting together an Advisory Board made up of your investors is a great way to provide professional proof to other investors or partners.

- Seek their guidance on strategic matters and problem-solving.

3. Exit Strategy

- Discuss potential exit strategies with angel investors, such as acquisition or IPO, and align expectations regarding the timeline for exits.

VII. Continuous Relationship Building

1. Building a Network: Continue networking with angel investors and other entrepreneurs even after securing investment.

2. Mentorship and Support: Cultivate mentorship relationships with angel investors to tap into their industry insights and experiences.

Navigating the world of angel investing involves building relationships, crafting compelling pitches, and understanding the intricacies of investment terms and equity. By presenting a strong business case and fostering positive investor relationships, you can secure the financial support and guidance you need to grow your startup.

3. Peer-to-Peer (P2P) Lending

Let's now dive into P2P lending platforms and how they can provide alternative financing. We'll explore strategies for securing loans from individual investors through online lending networks.

I. Understanding P2P Lending Platforms

1. Introduction to P2P Lending

Peer-to-Peer (P2P) lending platforms are online marketplaces that connect individuals or businesses in need of loans with individual investors willing to lend money.

2. How P2P Lending Works

- Entrepreneurs create loan listings on P2P platforms, specifying the amount they need, the interest rate they're willing to pay, and the loan's purpose.

- Individual investors review these listings and choose which loans to fund.

- Once the loan is fully funded, the entrepreneur receives the funds and repays the loan with interest over time.

II. Benefits of P2P Lending for Entrepreneurs

1. Access to Funding: P2P lending provides an alternative source of financing, especially for those who may not qualify for traditional bank loans.

2. Competitive Interest Rates: Interest rates on P2P loans can be competitive, often based on the borrower's creditworthiness and the perceived risk of the loan.

3. Quick Approval: P2P platforms often offer faster loan approval and disbursement compared to traditional lenders.

III. Strategies for Securing P2P Loans

1. Optimize Your Loan Listing

- Craft a compelling loan listing that clearly explains your business, the purpose of the loan, and how you plan to use the funds.

- Provide detailed financial projections and a repayment plan that instills confidence in potential investors.

2. Build a Strong Borrower Profile

- Invest time in building a robust borrower profile on the P2P platform. Highlight your business experience, achievements, and qualifications.

- Address any concerns or potential risks investors might have.

3. Diversify Loan Listings

- Consider diversifying your loan requests on multiple P2P lending platforms to increase your chances of securing funds.

4. Engage with Investors

- Actively engage with investors who express interest in your loan. Be responsive to their questions and concerns.

- Building a positive relationship can encourage investors to fund your loan.

5. Offer Collateral or Guarantees

- Some P2P platforms allow entrepreneurs to offer collateral or personal guarantees, which can make your loan listing more attractive to investors. Be careful, though—remember I lost a lot of money borrowing this way.

6. Leverage Social Proof

- If you have a strong network or social following, leverage it to promote your loan listing. Encourage friends, family, and supporters to invest. Many strong relationships have fallen out over this type of funding, so beware.

7. Provide Regular Updates

- Keep investors informed about your business's progress, achievements, and financial performance.

- Regular updates can build trust and confidence among your investors.

IV. Risks and Considerations

1. Interest Rates: Be prepared for varying interest rates, which can depend on your creditworthiness and the platform's policies.

2. Repayment Terms: Understand the repayment terms and schedules associated with your P2P loan.

3. Platform Fees: Be aware of any fees associated with P2P lending platforms, such as origination fees or servicing fees.

4. Default Risk: Consider the risk of not being able to repay the loan if your business faces challenges. Understand the potential consequences.

5. Regulatory Environment: Keep an eye on the regulatory environment for P2P lending in your region, as it can impact how these platforms operate.

P2P lending can be a viable financing option if you're seeking alternative funding sources. By implementing strategies and optimizing your loan listing, you can increase your chances of securing the necessary funds for your business while building a positive relationship with individual investors.

Here are some of the most popular P2P platforms:

- LendingClub: LendingClub is one of the largest and most recognized P2P lending platforms in the United States. It offers personal loans, business loans, and patient solutions.

- Prosper: Prosper is another prominent P2P lending platform in the U.S., facilitating personal loans for various purposes, including debt consolidation and home improvement.

- Funding Circle: Funding Circle is known for its focus on small business loans. It connects investors with small and medium-sized enterprises seeking financing.

- Zopa: Zopa is a UK-based P2P lending platform specializing in personal loans. It was one of the pioneers in the P2P lending industry.

- RateSetter: RateSetter, based in the UK, offers personal and business loans. It is known for its provision fund, which helps protect investors against borrower defaults.

- Upstart: Upstart is a P2P lending platform in the U.S. that uses artificial intelligence and machine learning to assess creditworthiness and offer personal loans.

- SoFi: SoFi, short for Social Finance, provides a range of financial products, including personal loans, student loan refinancing, and mortgages.

- Folk2Folk: Folk2Folk is a UK-based P2P lending platform specializing in secured business loans, particularly for rural and agricultural businesses.

- FundingSecure: FundingSecure, also in the UK, focuses on asset-backed lending, where borrowers provide collateral to secure their loans.

- Mintos: Mintos is a European P2P lending marketplace that offers loans from various loan originators across multiple countries. It focuses on personal loans, car loans, and more.

- Bondora: Bondora is an Estonian P2P lending platform that provides personal loans to borrowers across Europe.

- Twino: Twino is another European P2P lending platform offering consumer loans and investing opportunities to individuals.

Please keep in mind that the P2P lending landscape is dynamic, and the popularity and regulations of these platforms may change. Before using any P2P lending platform, it's essential to conduct thorough research, understand their terms and conditions, and consider the associated risks. Many come and go so consider this when working through the list I've provided.

Section 2: FinTech and Financial Management

Managing your finances is critical for long-term success. I'll introduce you to financial technology (FinTech) tools that streamline your financial operations. In this section, you'll learn how to create budgets, forecast future financial needs, and ensure your business's financial sustainability.

The Power of FinTech Tools:

1. Streamlining Financial Operations

Let's explore FinTech solutions that automate and simplify financial tasks such as invoicing, expense tracking, and payroll management. I'll delve into cloud-based accounting platforms that offer real-time insights into your financial health.

I. FinTech Solutions

1. Introduction to FinTech: FinTech refers to technology-driven financial innovations that streamline and improve financial services and operations.

2. Benefits of FinTech for Entrepreneurs: FinTech solutions can significantly benefit you by automating financial tasks, reducing manual work, and enhancing accuracy.

II. Automation of Financial Tasks

1. Invoicing Solutions: FinTech platforms like FreshBooks, QuickBooks, or Xero can automate invoicing processes. They allow you to create and send professional invoices to clients, set up recurring invoices, and track payment statuses.

2. Expense Tracking Tools: Tools like Expensify or Receipt Bank automate expense tracking. You can scan receipts, categorize expenses, and generate reports for better financial control.

3. Payroll Management Systems: FinTech solutions like Gusto or ADP streamline payroll processing. They automate calculations, tax filings, and direct deposits, reducing administrative burdens.

4. Financial Reporting Software: Financial reporting tools like Tableau or Power BI provide data visualization and reporting capabilities. They help entrepreneurs gain insights into their financial data for informed decision-making.

III. Cloud-Based Accounting Platforms

1. Real-Time Financial Insights: Cloud-based accounting platforms, such as QuickBooks Online, Xero, or Zoho Books, offer real-time access to financial data from any device with internet connectivity.

2. Automated Bank Feeds: These platforms can connect to your business bank accounts and credit cards, automatically importing transactions and ensuring data accuracy.

3. Collaboration and Accessibility: Cloud-based accounting platforms facilitate collaboration with accountants and team members. You can grant access and work together on financial tasks in real-time.

4. Integration with Other Tools: Many cloud-based accounting platforms integrate with other business tools, such

as payment processors and e-commerce platforms, streamlining data flow.

5. Scalability: These platforms are scalable, making them suitable for businesses of all sizes. You can add or remove features as your business grows.

6. Security and Data Backup: Cloud-based platforms often have robust security measures and automated data backup processes to protect your financial information.

IV. Features

1. Cash Flow Forecasting: Some platforms offer cash flow forecasting tools, helping entrepreneurs predict future financial trends and make proactive decisions.

2. Budgeting and Financial Planning: Many cloud-based systems have built-in budgeting and financial planning modules to help entrepreneurs set financial goals and track progress.

3. Tax Compliance: These platforms often integrate with tax preparation software to streamline tax compliance and reporting.

4. Mobile Apps: Mobile apps associated with these platforms allow you to manage finances on the go, improving flexibility.

FinTech solutions and cloud-based accounting platforms are invaluable for entrepreneurs seeking to simplify financial tasks, gain real-time insights, and ensure financial accuracy. These tools not only save time but also provide the data needed to make informed business decisions and maintain financial health.

2. Cash Flow Management

It's time to master cash flow management techniques using FinTech tools. We'll learn how to develop strategies to optimize cash flow, manage working capital, and ensure liquidity during both growth and challenging periods.

I. Cash Flow Management Techniques

Cash flow management involves monitoring and controlling the movement of money in and out of your business to ensure you have enough liquidity to cover expenses.

II. Using FinTech Tools for Cash Flow Management

1. Cash Flow Forecasting Tools: Utilize FinTech cash flow forecasting tools that allow you to project future cash flows based on historical data and anticipated income and expenses.

2. Real-Time Transaction Tracking: FinTech solutions can track and categorize transactions in real-time, providing you with an up-to-date view of your cash position.

3. Automation of Bill Payments: Automate recurring bill payments using FinTech platforms to ensure bills are paid on time while optimizing cash flow.

4. Expense Management: Implement expense management tools that help track and control spending, flagging excessive or unnecessary expenses.

III. Strategies to Optimize Cash Flow

1. Streamline Receivables: Accelerate receivables by offering discounts for early payments, sending automated payment reminders, and optimizing credit policies.

2. Manage Payables Efficiently: Negotiate favorable payment terms with suppliers and consider using dynamic discounting to take advantage of early payment discounts.

3. Inventory Management: Implement just-in-time inventory practices to reduce carrying costs and free up cash that would otherwise be tied up in inventory.

4. Debt Management: Optimize your debt structure by refinancing high-interest loans and considering lines of credit to bridge temporary cash shortfalls.

IV. Managing Working Capital

1. Working Capital Analysis: Regularly analyze your working capital, which is the difference between current assets and current liabilities. Ensure it remains positive.

2. Inventory Turnover: Aim for a healthy inventory turnover ratio by minimizing excess inventory and ensuring products move efficiently.

3. Receivables and Payables Days: Monitor the number of days it takes to collect receivables and pay payables. Strive to reduce both to optimize cash flow.

V. Liquidity Management

1. Emergency Fund: Maintain an emergency cash reserve to cover unexpected expenses or revenue shortfalls during challenging periods.

2. Line of Credit: Establish a line of credit with a financial institution that you can tap into when needed to maintain liquidity.

3. Cash Flow Stress Testing: Perform stress tests on your cash flow projections to assess how your business would withstand adverse scenarios.

VI. Continuous Monitoring and Adjustment

1. Regular Review: Continuously monitor your cash flow and adjust your strategies as needed. Regular reviews are essential for cash flow management.

2. Scenario Planning: Develop contingency plans for different scenarios, such as rapid growth, economic downturns, or unexpected disruptions.

VII. FinTech Solutions for Cash Flow

1. Software Selection

Choose FinTech cash flow management software that aligns with your business needs and integrates seamlessly with your financial systems.

The best cash flow management software for your business will depend on your specific needs, the size of your business, and your existing financial systems. Here are some popular cash flow management software options that offer various features and integration capabilities:

- QuickBooks: QuickBooks is a widely used accounting software that offers cash flow management features. It's suitable for small to medium-sized businesses and integrates seamlessly with various financial systems.

- Xero: Xero is another popular accounting software known for its cash flow forecasting and management capabilities. It's user-friendly and offers integrations with many financial apps and platforms. This is the one I use.

- Sage Intacct: Sage Intacct is a cloud-based financial management software designed for mid-sized and enterprise-level businesses. It offers robust cash flow management and forecasting features.

- Float: Float is a dedicated cash flow forecasting and management software. It integrates with accounting software like Xero and QuickBooks, making it suitable for businesses focused on cash flow.

- Dryrun: Dryrun is a cash flow forecasting tool that helps businesses create scenarios and visualize cash flow trends. It integrates with QuickBooks, Xero, and other accounting software.

- Pulse by Zoho: Zoho offers Pulse, a cash flow management tool that integrates with Zoho Books and other accounting software. It provides insights into cash flow patterns and helps with financial planning.

- Adaptive Insights: Adaptive Insights is a financial planning and analysis platform that includes cash flow forecasting and management capabilities. It's suitable for larger businesses and offers integration options.

- SAP Business ByDesign: SAP's Business ByDesign is an ERP solution that includes cash flow management features. It's designed for medium-sized businesses and offers integration with other SAP products.

- NetSuite: NetSuite is an ERP system that includes cash flow management as part of its financial management suite. It's suitable for medium-sized and enterprise-level businesses and offers extensive integration capabilities.

- TreasurEase: TreasurEase is a treasury management software designed for cash flow forecasting and optimization. It integrates with various financial systems and can be customized for specific needs.

When choosing cash flow management software, consider factors such as the size and complexity of your business, your budget, and the level of integration you require with existing financial systems. It's often helpful to take advantage of free trials or consultations offered by these software providers to determine which one aligns best with your business needs. Additionally, consult with your finance or accounting team to ensure the chosen software meets their requirements for effective cash flow management.

2. Training and Support

Invest in training for you and your team to effectively use FinTech tools for cash flow management.

Cash flow management, supported by FinTech tools, is essential for the financial health and sustainability of your business. By optimizing cash flow, managing working capital, and ensuring liquidity, you can navigate growth periods and overcome challenges with greater financial resilience.

3. Creating Strategic Budgets

I. Budgeting Techniques

Here we are going to outline basic budgeting techniques to use when setting up your new business:

1. Create a Startup Budget

- List all of your anticipated expenses, such as rent, utilities, equipment, marketing, salaries, and supplies.

- Estimate your revenue based on your business model, market research, and sales projections.

- Calculate the difference between total expenses and estimated revenue to determine whether your business will generate a profit or incur a loss.

2. Track Your Expenses

- Use accounting software or spreadsheets to monitor your expenses and revenue.

- Categorize expenses (e.g., marketing, rent, utilities) to understand where your money is going and identify areas for potential cost savings.

- Regularly review cash flow to ensure you have enough money to cover expenses.

3. Set Financial Goals

- Define both short-term (e.g., monthly, quarterly) and long-term (e.g., annual) financial goals for your business, such as revenue targets or cost reduction goals.

- Make goals specific and measurable to track progress and make adjustments as needed.

4. Build a Contingency Fund

- Set aside a portion of your budget as an emergency fund to cover unexpected expenses or revenue shortfalls.

- Having a financial cushion provides peace of mind and stability during challenging times.

5. Differentiate Between Needs and Wants

- Distinguish between essential expenses necessary for your business's survival and non-essential expenses that can be reduced or eliminated.

- Prioritize spending on critical areas of your business before discretionary spending.

6. Use Zero-Based Budgeting

- Start each budgeting cycle with a clean slate and allocate funds based on your business's current needs and priorities.

- Justify every expense, encouraging scrutiny and preventing unnecessary spending.

7. Review and Adjust Regularly

- Review your budget and financial statements monthly to ensure you're on track.

- Identify variances and adjust your spending or revenue strategies as needed.

- Create an annual budget to guide your financial plans for the year ahead.

8. Seek Professional Advice

- Consult with a financial professional, such as an accountant or financial advisor, to help create and manage your budget effectively.

9. Be Conservative with Revenue Projections

- When estimating revenue, be conservative to avoid overestimating income and potential budget shortfalls.

10. Prepare for Unforeseen Expenses

- Include a line item in your budget for unexpected expenses or contingencies to be prepared for unforeseen challenges.

Budgeting is an ongoing process that requires discipline and regular monitoring. By creating and following a budget, you can gain better control over your finances, make informed decisions, and work toward your business goals.

II. Rolling Forecasts

Creating rolling forecasts is a valuable financial management technique for new entrepreneurs. Rolling forecasts provide continuous insights into your financial future and allow you to adapt to changing circumstances. Here's how to create and use rolling forecasts:

1. Initial Budget: Start with an initial budget for your business. This is a detailed plan that includes revenue projections, expense estimates, and other financial metrics for a specific period, usually a year.

2. Set Forecasting Frequency: Decide on the frequency of your rolling forecasts. Common intervals are monthly or quarterly, but it can vary based on your business's needs.

3. Gather Real-Time Data: Continuously collect real-time financial data and market information. This includes sales

figures, expenses, inventory levels, and relevant industry trends. Use financial software or tools to streamline data collection.

4. Update Forecasts Regularly: At the end of each forecasting period (e.g., monthly or quarterly), update your budget and forecasts using the most recent data. This step is crucial for maintaining accuracy.

5. Adjust Assumptions: Review and, if necessary, adjust the assumptions and variables in your budget. For example, if you notice a decrease in sales, revise your revenue projections accordingly.

6. Analyze Variances: Compare your actual financial results to your rolling forecasts. Analyze any significant variances and investigate the reasons behind them. This helps in identifying areas that need attention.

7. Use Scenario Analysis: Conduct scenario analysis to explore different possible outcomes based on changing assumptions. For instance, create scenarios for best-case, worst-case, and most likely outcomes to assess your business's resilience.

8. Adjust Strategies: Based on your analysis and scenario planning, adjust your business strategies, such as marketing, pricing, or cost-cutting measures, to align with your financial goals.

9. Communicate with Stakeholders: Share your updated forecasts and any significant findings with key stakeholders, such as investors, partners, or employees. Transparent communication helps build trust.

10. Continuously Improve: Rolling forecasts are an iterative process. Continuously refine your forecasting techniques based on past performance and evolving business conditions.

Benefits of Rolling Forecasts:

- Agility: Rolling forecasts allow you to quickly adapt to changing market conditions and make informed decisions.

- Early Detection: They help in early detection of potential financial challenges, allowing you to take corrective actions promptly.

- Improved Decision-Making: With access to real-time data and insights, you can make more informed decisions that align with your business's financial goals.

- Resource Allocation: Rolling forecasts aid in optimizing resource allocation, ensuring that you allocate resources where they are most needed.

In summary, rolling forecasts are a dynamic financial management tool that empowers new entrepreneurs to stay agile, respond to market changes, and make data-driven decisions. By continuously updating your budget based on real-time data and market trends, you can improve your business's financial resilience and overall performance.

4. Financial Scenario Planning

Develop financial scenario planning models to prepare for various economic conditions and market fluctuations. This proactive approach enables you to adapt quickly to changing circumstances.

Financial Sustainability:

1. Profitability Analysis: Conduct profitability analysis to assess the true profitability of different product lines, customer segments, or geographic markets. Identify areas for optimization and growth.

2. Risk Management: Explore risk management strategies to protect your business from financial uncertainties. This includes assessing and mitigating risks related to market volatility, supply chain disruptions, and regulatory changes.

3. Investment Strategies: Learn investment strategies to maximize the return on your financial assets. This may involve diversifying your investment portfolio, considering alternative investments, or engaging in strategic mergers and acquisitions.

Chapter 8:
Legal Love and Care

Section 1: Choosing the Right Legal Structure

Choosing the right legal structure is a pivotal decision. I'll discuss the differences between sole proprietorship, LLCs, and corporations. You'll understand the legal responsibilities associated with each, making an informed choice for your business. I'll also explore the process of registering your business and obtaining necessary licenses.

1. Sole Proprietorship

- Ownership: A sole proprietorship is the simplest form of business structure and is owned by a single individual. The business and the owner are considered the same legal entity.

- Liability: The owner has unlimited personal liability for the business's debts and legal obligations. This means personal assets can be at risk to satisfy business debts or legal claims.

- Taxation: Income from the business is typically reported on the owner's personal tax return (Schedule C) and is subject to self-employment taxes.

- Registration and Licensing: In most cases, there is no formal registration required to start a sole proprietorship, but you may need to obtain local business licenses or permits depending on your location and industry.

2. LLC (Limited Liability Company) for the USA, for Australia we would call this a PTY Limited Co (Proprietary Limited Company)

- Ownership: An LLC is owned by one or more members (owners). Members can be individuals, other companies, or even other LLCs.

- Liability: The primary advantage of an LLC is that it offers limited liability to its members. This means personal assets are generally protected from business debts and legal claims.

- Taxation: LLCs offer flexibility in taxation. They can be taxed as a sole proprietorship (for single-member LLCs), a partnership (for multi-member LLCs), or elect to be taxed as a corporation (C-corp or S-corp). This allows members to choose the tax structure that best suits their needs.

- Legal Responsibilities: LLCs typically require the drafting of an operating agreement, which outlines the management structure, member roles, and decision-making processes. Compliance with state regulations and annual filings is also necessary in many cases.

- Registration and Licensing: To establish an LLC, you'll need to file articles of organization with the state in which you plan to operate. You may also need to obtain local business licenses or permits.

3. Corporations (C-Corp and S-Corp)

- Ownership: Corporations are owned by shareholders, and ownership is determined by the number of shares held.

- Liability: Shareholders generally have limited liability, meaning their personal assets are protected from the corporation's debts and legal obligations.

- Taxation:

    i. C-Corporation: Subject to double taxation, where the corporation is taxed on its profits, and shareholders are taxed on dividends received.

    ii. S-Corporation: Pass-through taxation, where the corporation's income and losses are passed through to shareholders, who report them on their personal tax returns.

- Legal Responsibilities: Corporations require more formalities and governance structures than sole proprietorships or LLCs. This includes holding regular shareholder meetings, keeping minutes, and maintaining corporate bylaws.

- Registration and Licensing: To establish a corporation, you'll need to file articles of incorporation with the state. You must also elect a board of directors, appoint officers, and follow state-specific regulations. Local business licenses may also be required.

Process of Registering and Licensing a Business

- Choose a Business Name: Ensure your chosen name is unique and compliant with state regulations. Check for trademark availability.

- Choose a Business Structure: Decide between a sole proprietorship, LLC, or corporation based on your needs and goals.

- Register with the State: File the necessary formation documents with the state, such as articles of organization (LLC) or articles of incorporation (corporation). Pay any required filing fees.

- Obtain an EIN: Apply for an Employer Identification Number (EIN) from the IRS; or in Australia, apply for a Business Registration Number (ABN) if your business structure requires it. This is often necessary for tax purposes and hiring employees.

- Comply with Local Regulations: Check with your local city or county government for any additional licenses or permits required for your specific location and industry.

- File Annual Reports: Keep up with any required annual filings and fees to maintain your business's good standing in the state.

- Consult with Professionals: Absolutely seek legal and financial advice from professionals to ensure compliance and proper business structuring.

Choosing the right business structure is a critical decision for any entrepreneur, as it affects legal liability, taxation, and operational flexibility. Consulting with a legal or financial advisor is recommended to make an informed choice based on your business goals and circumstances.

Section 2: Protecting Your Business

Protecting your intellectual property is crucial in today's world. I'll demystify trademarks, copyrights, and patents, helping you safeguard your ideas. Additionally, I'll delve into contract creation, ensuring your business interests are protected in agreements. Data privacy and security will also be discussed to protect your digital assets.

1. Trademarks, Copyrights, and Patents

- Trademarks: Trademarks protect your brand's identity, including logos, names, and slogans. Registering a trademark with the appropriate government agency (e.g., USPTO in the U.S. — look up the relevant agency in your country) gives you exclusive rights to use that mark and prevents others from using similar marks in your industry.

- Copyrights: Copyrights protect original creative works, such as writings, music, art, and software. As the creator, you automatically hold copyright to your work, but registering it provides additional legal protection and the ability to enforce your rights.

- Patents: Patents protect inventions and processes for a specific period, typically 20 years. There are different types of patents, including utility patents (for inventions) and design patents (for ornamental designs). To obtain a patent, you must apply with the relevant patent office (e.g., USPTO in the U.S.).

2. Contract Creation

- Importance: Contracts are legally binding agreements that outline the terms and conditions of business relationships. They help clarify expectations, protect your interests, and prevent disputes.

- Key Elements: A well-drafted contract should include clear and detailed terms, including parties involved, scope of work, payment terms, deadlines, dispute resolution mechanisms, and confidentiality clauses.

- Legal Counsel: Always consult with an attorney/lawyer who specializes in contract law to ensure your contracts are legally sound and protect your interests.

3. Data Privacy and Security

- Data Protection: Protecting customer and business data is crucial. Ensure compliance with data protection regulations such as GDPR (in Europe) or CCPA (in California). As this is a global book, you'll need to look up the relevant agency in your country. Implement data security measures like encryption, access controls, and regular audits.

- Cybersecurity: Invest in robust cybersecurity measures to safeguard your digital assets from data breaches and cyberattacks. Regularly update software, use strong passwords, and educate employees about security best practices.

- Data Backup: Regularly back up essential data and ensure disaster recovery plans are in place to minimize data loss in case of unexpected events.

- Privacy Policies: Develop and prominently display clear privacy policies on your website, explaining how you collect, store, and use customer data.

- Employee Training: Train your team on data security and privacy practices to prevent accidental data leaks.

- Incident Response Plan: Develop a plan for responding to data breaches or security incidents, including communication with affected parties and regulatory authorities.

Remember that IP protection, contract creation, and data privacy are ongoing processes. As your business grows and evolves, revisit and update these measures to adapt to changing circumstances and legal requirements. Consulting with legal and cybersecurity professionals is advisable to ensure comprehensive protection for your business and digital assets. In fact, consider these professionals to be a crucial part of your team.

Section 3: Registering Your Business

I. Business Name Registration

Here we'll explore the process of selecting and registering your business name, including considerations related to trademarks and domain names.

1. Brainstorm and Choose a Business Name

- Start by brainstorming potential business names. Consider names that are unique, memorable, and relevant to your business's products or services.

- Ensure the name aligns with your brand identity and conveys the right message to your target audience.

- Check the availability of domain names (website addresses) associated with your chosen business name.

2. Research Trademark Availability

- Perform a thorough trademark search to check if your chosen name is already registered or in use by another business in your industry. You can use online trademark databases or consult with a trademark attorney for a comprehensive search.

- Ensure that your chosen name doesn't infringe on any existing trademarks, as this could lead to legal disputes in the future.

3. Register Your Business Name

Depending on your business structure, you'll follow different registration processes:

- Sole Proprietorship: You may not be required to register a business name if you're operating under your legal name. However, if you use a fictitious business name (also known as a "doing business as" or DBA name), you may need to register it with your local government or county.

- LLC or Corporation: If you're forming an LLC or corporation, you'll typically register your business name when you file the necessary formation documents with your state's business registration agency. Each state has its own process and requirements for business name registration.

4. Domain Name Registration

- Purchase a domain name that matches or closely aligns with your business name. Ideally, your domain name should be short, easy to remember, and reflective of your brand.

- Register your domain name with a reputable domain registrar. Consider securing variations of your domain name to protect your online presence. I use GoDaddy which has been a great platform and they have templates to get a website up and ready asap.

5. Legal Considerations

- Consult with a legal professional, such as an attorney/lawyer specializing in business law, to ensure that your chosen business name complies with all relevant regulations and doesn't infringe on existing trademarks.

6. Business Name Protection

- After registering your business name, consider applying for a trademark to protect your brand identity. This can provide legal protection against others using a similar name in your industry.

7. Use Consistently

- Once you have your business name and domain, use them consistently across all your branding, marketing materials, and online platforms to establish a strong brand presence.

8. Monitor for Trademark Violations

- Regularly monitor your business name to ensure no one else is using it without permission. If you discover trademark violations, take appropriate legal action to protect your intellectual property.

Remember that the process of selecting and registering a business name can vary depending on your location and business structure. It's essential to research and comply with your specific state and country's regulations to ensure a smooth and legally compliant registration process. Consulting with legal professionals can help you navigate any complex issues related to your business name.

II. Entity Formation

Here's a step-by-step guidance on forming your chosen legal structure, including filing articles of incorporation or organization, drafting operating agreements, and obtaining an employer identification number (EIN) or ABN (Australian Business Number). I know this is a slight repeat on what we covered earlier in this chapter, but we will dive a little deeper.

1. Determine Your Business Structure

Decide on the legal structure that best suits your business needs. Common options include:

- Sole Proprietorship

- Limited Liability Company (LLC)

- Corporation (C-Corp or S-Corp)

- Partnership

- Nonprofit Organization

2. File Articles of Incorporation or Organization

Depending on your chosen structure, you'll need to file specific formation documents:

- LLC: File Articles of Organization (or a similar document) with your state's Secretary of State office.

- Corporation: File Articles of Incorporation with your state's Secretary of State office.

- Partnership: Draft a partnership agreement that outlines the roles, responsibilities, and profit-sharing arrangements among partners. This is a crucial step for partnerships but doesn't require formal state filing.

3. Draft Operating Agreements or Bylaws

For LLCs and corporations, it's essential to create internal governance documents:

- LLC: Draft an Operating Agreement that outlines the management structure, member roles, and operating procedures.

- Corporation: Create Corporate Bylaws specifying how the business will be governed, including roles of officers and directors.

4. Obtain an Employer Identification Number (EIN) or Australian Business Number (ABN)

- An EIN, also known as a Federal Tax Identification Number or ABN (Australian Business Number) or the appropriate entity in your country. This is necessary for tax purposes and opening a business bank account.

- Apply for an EIN from the IRS online or by submitting Form SS-4; or in Australia, apply for an ABN online. It's typically a straightforward process.

5. Register for State and Local Taxes

- Depending on your location and business activities, you may need to register for state and local taxes, such as sales tax or employment tax.

- Check with your state's Department of Revenue or Taxation for specific requirements.

6. Comply with Regulatory Requirements: Research and adhere to industry-specific regulations, licensing requirements, and permits. Different businesses may have unique compliance needs.

7. Open a Business Bank Account: Separate your personal and business finances by opening a dedicated business bank account. This simplifies accounting and helps protect your personal assets.

8. Obtain Necessary Permits and Licenses: Identify and secure any required permits or licenses, such as health permits, occupational licenses, or industry-specific certifications.

9. Insure Your Business: Explore insurance options, including liability insurance, property insurance, and workers' compensation, depending on your business type. Reach out to an insurance broker like AON to help you with determining what insurance cover you need for your business type.

10. Keep Accurate Records: Maintain detailed financial records, contracts, and important business documents. Consider using accounting software as recommended earlier in this book to streamline record-keeping.

11. Comply with Ongoing Reporting Requirements: Stay compliant with ongoing reporting and filing requirements, such as annual reports, tax filings, and other regulatory obligations specific to your business structure and location.

12. Seek Legal and Accounting Advice: Consult with legal and accounting professionals to ensure that your business formation and compliance efforts are accurate and legally sound. I can't stress enough how important this is.

Starting a business involves various legal and regulatory steps that can vary by location and business type. Consulting with professionals, such as attorneys/lawyers and accountants, can help you navigate the complexities and ensure that you meet all legal requirements.

III. Licenses and Permits

Here we'll understand the types of licenses and permits your business may require, depending on your location and industry. Learn how to navigate the application process and maintain compliance.

1. Professional and Occupational Licenses

- Purpose: Certain professions, such as doctors, lawyers, electricians, and plumbers, require specific professional licenses.

- Application Process: Contact the relevant state or licensing board for your profession. Complete required education or exams, submit an application, and pay fees.

- Compliance: Keep your license current by renewing it as needed, fulfilling continuing education requirements, and adhering to professional standards.

2. Health Department Permits

- Purpose: Businesses in the food service, hospitality, or healthcare industry may require health department permits for safety and hygiene compliance.

- Application Process: Contact your local health department or agency responsible for regulating your industry. Meet food safety or health standards, complete an application, and schedule inspections if necessary.

- Compliance: Maintain cleanliness and adhere to health regulations to pass routine inspections and renew permits as required.

3. Zoning Permits

- Purpose: Zoning permits ensure that your business location complies with local zoning regulations and land use restrictions.

- Application Process: Contact your local zoning or planning department to determine zoning requirements and application procedures.

- Compliance: Operate your business within the zoning regulations for your location and obtain necessary variances or approvals if needed.

4. Environmental Permits

- Purpose: Businesses involved in activities that impact the environment, such as manufacturing or waste disposal, may require environmental permits.

- Application Process: Contact the appropriate environmental agency or department to determine the permits needed and the application process.

- Compliance: Implement environmentally friendly practices, follow permit conditions, and submit required reports or fees as specified.

5. Federal and State Business Licenses

- Purpose: Certain industries, such as alcohol production or transportation, require federal or state licenses.

- Application Process: Identify the federal or state agency responsible for your industry and follow their application process.

- Compliance: Maintain compliance with federal or state regulations, report regularly, and renew licenses as needed.

6. Home Occupation Permits

- Purpose: If you operate a business from your home, you may need a home occupation permit to comply with local zoning regulations.

- Application Process: Contact your local zoning department and inquire about home-based business regulations and permit requirements.

- Compliance: Follow the guidelines for home-based businesses, and renew the permit as necessary.

Navigating the application process for licenses and permits can be complex, so it's essential to research requirements specific to your location and industry. To maintain compliance, keep detailed records of your permits, renewal dates, and compliance obligations. Regularly review and update your permits to ensure you meet changing regulations and maintain legal status. Consulting with local government offices and industry-specific associations can provide valuable guidance.

Chapter 9:
Scaling and Blossoming

Leveraging Technology for Growth

Technology can supercharge your business. I'll explore how to use technology to scale your operations efficiently.

1. E-Commerce Solutions

- Select an e-commerce platform that offers features tailored to your business needs. Consider options like Shopify Plus, Magento Commerce, or WooCommerce with customized plugins.

- Implement a responsive and mobile-friendly design to cater to a broader audience.

- Leverage features such as one-click checkout, subscription models, and personalized product recommendations to enhance the customer experience.

- Utilize e-commerce analytics to track customer behavior, cart abandonment, and sales funnel performance.

2. Marketing Automation

- Invest in marketing automation platforms like Marketo, HubSpot Marketing Hub, or Salesforce Pardot. These tools allow you to create sophisticated marketing workflows and nurture leads effectively.

- Implement lead scoring to prioritize and segment leads based on their engagement and behavior.

- Utilize dynamic content and personalized email campaigns to engage customers at different stages of the buyer's journey.

3. Artificial Intelligence (AI) and Machine Learning (ML)

- Explore AI and ML applications for your business, such as chatbots, predictive analytics, and recommendation engines.

- Implement chatbots to provide real-time customer support and answer common inquiries.

- Use predictive analytics to forecast demand, optimize pricing, and improve inventory management.

- Leverage recommendation engines to suggest relevant products to customers, increasing cross-selling and upselling opportunities.

4. Workflow Automation

- Identify repetitive tasks in your business processes and automate them using workflow automation platforms like Zapier, Integromat, or Microsoft Power Automate.

- Automate data entry, document routing, and approvals to streamline internal operations.

- Integrate various software tools to create seamless workflows and eliminate manual data entry errors.

5. Customer Relationship Management (CRM) Enhancements

- Enhance your CRM system with features such as AI-driven lead scoring, predictive analytics, and social media integration.

- Use AI to analyze customer data and identify potential leads that match your ideal customer profile.

- Integrate social media data to gain a 360-degree view of customer interactions and sentiments.

6. Analytics and Business Intelligence (BI)

- Deploy analytics tools like Tableau, Looker, or QlikView to gain deeper insights into your business data.

- Create custom dashboards and reports that provide real-time visibility into key performance indicators (KPIs).

- Use AI-powered analytics to uncover hidden patterns and trends within your data.

7. Mobile Commerce Optimization

- Optimize your mobile e-commerce experience by focusing on mobile app development, progressive web apps (PWAs), and mobile-responsive design.

- Implement features like in-app messaging, mobile wallets, and location-based services to enhance user engagement.

- Utilize mobile analytics to track user behavior and preferences on mobile devices.

8. Cybersecurity and Data Protection

- Prioritize cybersecurity with measures like multi-factor authentication (MFA), penetration testing, and intrusion detection systems.

- Invest in data protection solutions, including encryption, data loss prevention (DLP), and regular security audits to safeguard customer data.

9. Customer Personalization

- Implement personalization techniques, including AI-driven product recommendations, dynamic pricing, and content personalization.

- Use predictive analytics to anticipate customer needs and deliver tailored experiences.

By harnessing these technology techniques, you can not only scale your business efficiently but also gain a competitive edge in today's rapidly evolving digital landscape. Always stay informed about emerging technologies and industry trends to adapt and thrive in the digital era.

Chapter 10:
The Power of Resilience

Section 1: Building Resilience

Resilience is your secret weapon against adversity. Cultivate a growth mindset, learn from failures, and discover stress management techniques. I'll explore the importance of taking care of yourself as you navigate the ups and downs of entrepreneurship.

1. Cultivating a Growth Mindset

- Definition: A growth mindset is the belief that abilities and intelligence can be developed through dedication, hard work, and learning from mistakes.

- Importance: Embracing a growth mindset encourages resilience, adaptability, and a willingness to take on challenges.

- Strategies:

    i.   Embrace challenges as opportunities for growth rather than obstacles.

    ii. View failures as learning experiences and focus on improvement.

iii. Continuously seek learning and development opportunities through books, courses, and mentorship.

iv. Surround yourself with supportive individuals who share a growth mindset.

2. Learning from Failures

- Embrace Failure: Understand that failure is a natural part of the entrepreneurial journey and an opportunity for growth. I've learned more from the introspection done on the sleepless nights I endured during failures than I ever did in the comfort of a good night's sleep enjoyed during periods of thriving.

- Reflect and Analyze: After a setback, take time to reflect on what went wrong, what could have been done differently, and what lessons can be drawn. Most entrepreneurs have to deal with failure at some stage of their careers. What's important is that you have to dust yourself off and keep going.

- Adapt and Pivot: Use the insights gained from failures to make informed decisions, adjust strategies, and pivot when necessary.

- Resilience: Develop resilience by staying determined and motivated despite setbacks.

3. Stress Management Techniques

- Identify Stressors: Recognize the sources of stress in your entrepreneurial journey, whether they're related to workload, financial pressures, or uncertainty.

- Time Management: Prioritize tasks and manage your time efficiently to reduce stress associated with overwhelm.

- Physical Activity: Regular exercise releases endorphins, reducing stress and enhancing overall well-being. I know that everyone preaches this and there's a reason for that—because it's true!

- Meditation and Mindfulness: Practice meditation and mindfulness techniques to calm your mind, improve focus, and reduce anxiety. We covered these techniques in earlier chapters.

- Healthy Lifestyle: Maintain a balanced diet, get adequate sleep, and avoid excessive caffeine or alcohol consumption.

- Support Network: Seek support from friends, family, mentors or professional counselors to discuss and manage stress effectively.

4. Importance of Self-Care

- Physical Well-Being: Prioritize your physical health by maintaining a balanced diet, exercising regularly, and getting enough rest.

- Mental Health: Pay attention to your mental well-being by managing stress, seeking therapy or counseling when needed, and practicing self-compassion.

- Work-Life Balance: Set boundaries between work and personal life to avoid burnout. Dedicate time to hobbies, relaxation, and spending quality moments with loved ones.

- Continuous Learning: Invest in your personal and professional growth through reading, courses, workshops, and networking events.

- Delegation: Delegate tasks and responsibilities to prevent overburdening yourself and allow for more focus on strategic aspects of your business. We covered the technology tools available to us now to free up our time to devote to self-care.

Understanding that entrepreneurship is a journey filled with ups and downs, and actively working on personal growth and self-care, can significantly contribute to your success. A growth mindset, resilience, and effective stress management techniques will empower you to navigate the challenges and uncertainties of entrepreneurship with confidence and well-being.

Section 2: Adapting and Thriving

Change is the only constant in the business world, and your ability to adapt is a key factor in your success. Change is inevitable, and I'll show you how to embrace it. In this chapter, we will explore techniques that will help you not only survive but also thrive in the ever-evolving business landscape. You'll learn how to pivot your business model when necessary, stay nimble in response to market shifts, and harness the power of change to drive your business forward.

1. Continuous Market Analysis

- Stay Informed: Regularly monitor market trends, customer preferences, and emerging technologies that could impact your industry.

- Competitor Analysis: Study your competitors to identify their strategies and potential gaps you can exploit.

- Customer Feedback: Collect and analyze customer feedback to understand their evolving needs and expectations.

2. Agile Business Model

- Agile Principles: Implement agile principles within your organization, emphasizing adaptability and responsiveness.

- Cross-Functional Teams: Create cross-functional teams capable of making rapid decisions and adjustments.

- Iterative Approach: Adopt an iterative approach to product development, allowing for frequent updates and improvements.

- Feedback Loops: Establish feedback loops with customers, enabling real-time adjustments based on their input.

3. Pivoting Strategies

- Recognizing Signs: Be vigilant for signs that your current business model may no longer be effective, such as declining sales or shifts in customer behavior.

- Data-Driven Decisions: Rely on data and market research to inform your pivot strategy. Avoid making hasty decisions based solely on intuition.

- Testing and Validation: When considering a pivot, test new strategies or product ideas on a smaller scale to validate their potential before a full-scale rollout.

- Communication: Effectively communicate changes to your team and stakeholders to ensure alignment and understanding.

4. Innovation Culture

- Encourage Creativity: Foster a culture of innovation where employees feel encouraged to propose new ideas and solutions.

- Experimentation: Allow for controlled experimentation and risk-taking, understanding that not every idea will succeed.

- Learning from Failure: Emphasize that failure is a part of the innovation process, as long as it leads to valuable insights.

5. Strategic Partnerships

- Collaborative Partnerships: Forge strategic partnerships with other businesses and entrepreneurs that can complement your offerings or provide access to new markets.

- Joint Ventures: Explore joint ventures or alliances to share resources and risks in the face of significant industry changes.

- Acquisitions: Consider acquisitions of startups or companies that align with your evolving business goals.

6. Customer-Centric Approach

- Customer-Centered Innovation: Focus on meeting customer needs and solving their problems, even if it means changing your business model.

- Feedback Integration: Integrate customer feedback into your product development process to ensure that changes align with their preferences.

7. Agility in Operations

- Supply Chain Flexibility: Maintain flexible supply chains that can adapt to shifts in demand, sourcing, or production.

- Inventory Management: Implement just-in-time inventory management to reduce storage costs and adapt to changing product demand.

8. Change Management

- Employee Training: Train and educate your employees to embrace change and adapt to new processes and technologies.

- Leadership Support: Leadership should lead by example, showing enthusiasm and commitment to change initiatives.

9. Scenario Planning

- Scenario Analysis: Develop various scenarios for potential changes in the market and create strategies to address each scenario.

- Contingency Plans: Have contingency plans in place to respond swiftly to unexpected disruptions.

Mastering these techniques for embracing change and thriving amid uncertainty will not only help you survive in dynamic markets but also position your business for long-term success. Remember that change is a constant in the business world, and those who adapt and innovate tend to thrive.

Chapter 11:
Sisterhood and Support

Section 1: The Power of Female Networks

Find your tribe! I'll explore the value of women-focused entrepreneurial communities. Discover how connecting with like-minded women can provide support, inspiration, and collaboration opportunities. Together, we can lift each other up.

1. Supportive Environment

Shared Experiences: Women in entrepreneurship often face unique challenges and opportunities. Being part of a women-focused community allows you to connect with others who understand and can relate to these experiences. Here are some of the challenges unique to female founders that you should be aware of.

Female founders may encounter unique challenges in the business world due to gender-related biases and societal expectations. Here are some of the challenges they may face:

- Access to Funding: Women often have a harder time accessing funding for their startups. Investors, especially male investors, may exhibit unconscious biases that lead them to invest less in female-led businesses.

- Network Disparities: Many industries have predominantly male networks, which can make it challenging for female founders to build connections and access mentors or advisors.

- Gender Bias: Gender bias can affect how women are perceived in leadership roles. Some may question a female founder's competence or leadership abilities more than they would a male counterpart's.

- Work-Life Balance: Women may feel additional pressure to balance family and work responsibilities. This can be especially challenging for startup founders who often work long hours.

- Mentorship and Role Models: The lack of female role models and mentors in entrepreneurship can make it difficult for women to find guidance and support.

- Imposter Syndrome: Women may be more susceptible to imposter syndrome, doubting their own accomplishments and feeling like they don't deserve their success.

- Pitching and Negotiation: Female founders might face challenges in pitching and negotiation. Some studies suggest that women who negotiate assertively can be perceived as aggressive.

- Access to Resources: Women may have limited access to resources and opportunities, including business networks, education, and training.

- Market Bias: In certain markets, there may be a bias against products or services designed by and for women.

It's important to note that despite these challenges, many female founders have successfully built thriving businesses. Overcoming these obstacles often requires resilience, seeking out supportive networks and mentorship, and challenging stereotypes and biases. The business world is becoming increasingly diverse and inclusive, and female entrepreneurs play a vital role in driving innovation and economic growth.

- Empowerment: Interacting with women who have overcome obstacles and achieved success can be incredibly empowering. It reminds you that you can accomplish your goals, too.

- Mentorship: Many women-focused communities offer mentorship programs where experienced entrepreneurs guide and advise those just starting out.

2. Inspiration and Role Models

- Role Models: Seeing other women succeed in entrepreneurship can be inspiring and provide you with role models to look up to. It helps you envision what's possible.

- Encouragement: Hearing stories of women who have overcome adversity to achieve their dreams can boost your confidence and motivation. There are some great Facebook groups for female founders that you should join to stay aware of events that are a good place for you to make connections.

3. Collaboration Opportunities

- Networking: Women-focused communities often provide opportunities to network and connect with fellow entrepreneurs. These connections can lead to collaborations, partnerships, and business opportunities.

- Skill Exchange: Collaboration within the community allows you to tap into a diverse range of skills and expertise, strengthening your business.

4. Access to Resources

- Resources and Education: Women-focused communities often offer workshops, webinars, and resources tailored to the unique needs of female entrepreneurs. This can help you acquire new skills and knowledge.

- Funding Opportunities: Some communities have connections to investors or funding opportunities specifically designed to support women-owned businesses.

5. Safe Space for Discussion

- Open Dialogue: These communities provide a safe and open space where you can discuss challenges, seek advice, and share your experiences without judgment.

- Feedback and Validation: It's a place to test your ideas, gain feedback, and receive validation for your business concepts.

6. Breaking Stereotypes

- Promoting Equality: Women-focused communities work towards breaking gender stereotypes in entrepreneurship and advocating for gender equality.

- Empowering Future Generations: By being part of such communities, you contribute to creating a more inclusive environment for the next generation of female entrepreneurs.

7. Market Insights

- Understanding Female Consumers: Being part of a women-focused community can give you insights into the preferences and needs of female consumers, a valuable market segment.

8. Building Confidence

- Public Speaking and Leadership Opportunities: Many women-focused communities encourage members to take on leadership roles and speak at events, helping you build confidence and visibility in your field.

In summary, women-focused entrepreneurial communities offer a nurturing and empowering environment where you can find support, inspiration, and collaboration opportunities. They help you navigate the unique challenges of entrepreneurship while providing a platform to thrive and make meaningful connections with like-minded women.

Section 2: Seeking Mentorship and Giving Back

Mentorship is a powerful tool for personal and professional growth. Learn how to find a mentor who resonates with your journey and goals. I'll also encourage you to pay it forward by becoming a mentor yourself, contributing to the employment of the next generation of female entrepreneurs.

Finding a Mentor:

1. Define Your Goals

- Know What You Need: Clarify your goals and what you hope to achieve with a mentor. Are you seeking guidance on a specific aspect of your business, personal development, or a combination of both?

2. Identify Potential Mentors

- Networking: Attend industry events, conferences, and women-focused entrepreneurial gatherings. These are great places to meet potential mentors.

- Online Communities: Join online communities, forums, and social media groups related to entrepreneurship and women in business. These platforms can help you connect with experienced entrepreneurs.

3. Research and Reach Out

- Learn About Potential Mentors: Research the background, experiences, and achievements of potential mentors. Ensure they align with your goals and values.

- Personalized Approach: When reaching out to someone, craft a personalized message that explains why you admire their work and how you believe their guidance would benefit your journey.

4. Be Open to Various Types of Mentors

- Peer Mentoring: Consider peer mentoring where you collaborate with someone at a similar stage of entrepreneurship. You can learn a lot from each other's experiences.

- Reverse Mentoring: Don't overlook the value of learning from younger entrepreneurs or individuals with different perspectives. Mentorship can be a two-way street.

5. Build the Relationship

- Regular Communication: Once you've found a mentor, establish regular communication. This might include meetings, phone calls, or emails.

- Set Clear Expectations: Be clear about your goals and what you hope to gain from the mentorship. Also, ask your mentor about their expectations.

6. Be a Good Mentee

- Show Gratitude: Express appreciation for your mentor's time and guidance.

- Be Open to Feedback: Be open to constructive criticism and feedback. It's an opportunity for growth.

7. Paying It Forward

i.   Gain Experience and Expertise

- **Continued Growth:** As you progress in your entrepreneurial journey, you'll gain valuable experience and expertise.

- **Identify Opportunities:** Recognize opportunities to share your knowledge and help others facing challenges you've already overcome.

ii.   Seek Opportunities to Mentor

- **Participate in Programs:** Join mentorship programs or organizations that facilitate mentorship matches.

- **Offer Your Help:** Let others in your network know that you're open to mentoring. Share your expertise and experiences.

iii.   Be an Active Listener

- **Understand Their Goals:** When mentoring, take the time to understand your mentee's goals, challenges, and aspirations.

- **Provide Guidance:** Offer guidance, insights, and advice based on your experiences.

iv.   Encourage and Empower

- **Boost Confidence:** Encourage your mentee to believe in themselves and their abilities.

- **Share Resources:** Provide resources, reading materials, and connections that can help your mentee on their journey.

v.   Create a Supportive Environment

- Safe Space: Foster a safe and open environment where your mentee feels comfortable discussing challenges and seeking advice.

By finding a mentor who resonates with your goals and experiences, and later becoming a mentor yourself, you contribute to the growth and empowerment of the next generation of female entrepreneurs. Mentorship is a powerful way to build a supportive community and drive positive change in the entrepreneurial landscape.

Conclusion

Congratulations on completing *FoundHER*, the essential business book for new female founders! With newfound knowledge, fresh insights, and a network of supportive entrepreneurs, you're equipped to embark on your entrepreneurial journey. Remember, it's not just about reaching your destination but also enjoying the adventures along the way. Your creativity, determination, and support system will propel you toward entrepreneurial success. Here's to your dreams and the incredible journey ahead.

x Melissa

Acknowledgements

A special thank-you must go to my book editor, formatter, and self-publishing wizard: Sangeet Pandey. If you're a publishing disrupter like me, you can contact her at sangeet2x@gmail.com

I really do want to thank the women I am proud to call my friends, who are successful entrepreneurs and whose daily grind inspires my own hustle.

To my son Jonah, you've inspired me to be the best version of myself, every day since the day I knew I was your incubator and you burst into my life.

To my daughter, Saskia. The way you look up to me will always make me stand just a little taller. You and your brother will always be my reasons for being.